PRAYING

THE LORD'S PRAYER

CLEDDIE KEITH

Destiny Image₀ Publishers, Inc.
P.O. Box 310
Shippensburg, PA 17257-0310

"Speaking to the Purposes of God for This Generation
and for the Generations to Come"

ISBN 0-7684-2249-3

For Worldwide Distribution
Printed in the U.S.A.

This book and all other Destiny Image, Revival Press, MercyPlace, Fresh Bread, Destiny Image Fiction, and Treasure House books are available at Christian bookstores and distributors worldwide.

1 2 3 4 5 6 7 8 9 10 / 10 09 08 07 06 05 04

For a U.S. bookstore nearest you, call 1-800-722-6774.
For more information on foreign distributors, call 717-532-3040.
Or reach us on the Internet:
www.destinyimage.com

Dedication

It is said, "You know a lot about a man by those who call him their friend." This book is prayerfully dedicated to my friends. They have been used by God to enlarge my life. They know who they are and how important they are to me.

Vernel Perry has defined by his life the true value of friendship. When I was young I asked God to give me lifetime friends to walk with me in ministry. Vernel was an answer to that prayer. He has been a, "Thy will be done in my life."

Endorsement

"Cleddie has done a wonderful job addressing the subject of prayer without being boring or religious. In reading this book you will gain practical insights and understanding. But more importantly you will find yourself drawn into his journey, sharing in his passion for God. Will you end up praying more? Yes, but this time out of delight and not mere duty."

Bill Johnson

Contents

The Lord's Prayer in the Ancient Aramaic language
Avvon d-bish-maiya, nith-qaddash shim-mukh.
Tih-teh mal-chootukh. Nih-weh çiw-yanukh:
ei-chana d'bish-maiya: ap b'ar-ah.
Haw lan lakh-ma d'soonqa-nan yoo-mana.
O'shwooq lan kho-bein:
ei-chana d'ap kh'nan shwiq-qan l'khaya-ween.
Oo'la te-ellan l'niss-yoona:
il-la paç-çan min beesha.
Mid-til de-di-lukh hai mal-choota oo khai-la oo tush-bookh-ta
l'alam al-mein. Aa-meen.

Galilean transliteration of The Lord's Prayer

"Therefore, this is how you shall pray:
'Our heavenly Father, hallowed is Your name.
Your Kingdom is come. Your will is done,
As in heaven so also on earth.
Give us the bread for our daily need.
And leave us serene,
just as we also allowed others serenity.
And do not pass us through trial,
except separate us from the evil one.
For Yours is the Kingdom, the Power and the Glory
To the end of the universe, of all the universes.'" Amen!

Foreword

Cleddie Keith is not only one of the great pastors of our time, but one who has a sense of history, particularly of the great prayer revivals - past and present. This valuable book gives a fresh approach to the greatest prayer pattern of all time, The Lord's Prayer. This is a valuable tool that has the ability to ignite a fresh revival of prayer throughout the world.

Pastor Cleddie is a man of prayer and has surrounded himself with people of prayer. I do not know any of his inner circle of friends that are not mighty prayer warriors themselves. Over the years, Pastor Keith has made it a point to know, personally, leaders of the prayer movement worldwide. This book not only presents the pattern of prayer taught by Jesus, but imparts a quest for revival that will come only when people pray.

I love Pastor Cleddie Keith and deeply appreciate the mark he has left on me personally and, the thousands of people with whom he has made contact in ministry around the world.

This book is a winner.

Dr. Bob Rodgers
Sr. Pastor, Evangel World Prayer Center
Louisville, Kentucky

Foreword

Cleddie Keith, like other anointed men of God, grew up with that well-known dictum: "No Christian is greater than his prayer life." His wide and effective ministry is due to the fact that he prays. God is at the center of his life. He is a God-intoxicated man.

Only a man who prays could give us a good book on prayer. These pages ring true. This is because the person who penned them speaks of God's power and presence in every personal conversation—in almost every sentence.

Cleddie sees prayer as both a privilege and an opporunity. I once had a friend who saw prayer as work. It was a task at times, albeit enjoyable.

But Cleddie's praying is quite like Enoch's, the seventh man from Adam. The Word says "he walked with God." He knew the pleasure of God's company. Communion was certainly no task for that saint of old. The Book of Hebrews tells us that Enoch's "pleased God." Cleddie sees prayer as both pleasing to God and pleasurable to the praying person. He enjoys God.

Still, for Cleddie prayer is more than a privilege. It is an opportunity to advance the Kingdom of Christ. It is the overthrowing and plundering of satan's kingdom.

How do we arrive at this kind of effective praying? How do we approach God? Cleddie provides a pracical and encouraging teaching on how we can go farther on our knees; farther than we've been before. Cleddie reminds us that everything you do for the Lord matters, especially prayer.

Cleddie has listened to giants over the years. He has sat at the feet of great prayer warriors. The pages of his book are filled with poignant and inspirational quotations. But this is more than a good book on prayer. Cleddie opens to us his prayer life. His ministry ranges from the poor and broken in Houston's East End, to wealthy business and political leaders.

Prayer, like many of life's untimate privilages, cannot easily be analyzed; however, you can see its results. The life of prayer Cleddie teaches is a life of purpose and results. No spiritual soldier should go out to war before reading this book.

Robert Summers
Dallas, Texas
Prayer Mountain
Mountain Creek Community Church

Introduction

The sun had just peeked above the horizon that Wednesday morning in Louisville, Kentucky as I stepped into the sanctuary of the Evangelical World Prayer Center where my dear friends Bob and Margaret Rodgers are the senior pastors. The lights in the building were low, but there was a heartwarming roar of intercession reverberating throughout the room like the sound of a jet prepping before takeoff. Several hundred believers had gathered for prayer that morning, and a tangible spirit of prayer was heavy upon us. It was easy to see why this church was known as the church that prayer built. In front of me, I noticed an associate pastor on the platform leading the congregation in one point of the Lord's Prayer. My heart was deeply stirred by what I saw and heard. Intent worshippers gathered from throughout that region to pray at 6:00 am, hungry for a genuine manifestation of God. Their hearts were set on *prayer revival*. Ours must be as well. I believe that God is calling His Church to battle, and this means God is calling His Church to prayer.

PRAYING THE LORD'S PRAYER

Prayer must be passionate, and godly men of old knew this to be a truth. Professor Franklin Giddings loved to tell his sociology classes how, when he was a cub reporter, he had attended one of D.L. Moody's revival services. He marched with hundreds of others into an after-meeting for prayer. Moody, suspecting his real purpose, pointed his finger at young Giddings and said, "Young man, leave this room. You are not here to pray."[1] Moody knew the value of prayer.

In the last twenty years, I have seldom been to a church that does not participate in some form of "pattern praying." What we call *The Lord's Prayer* is often their weapon of choice. I have oftentimes joined with friends and family in praying The Lord's Prayer and have repeatedly found it to be much like a mirror that reveals my innermost heart and motives. It is a great tragedy that so many in the Church do not really understand the magnitude and meaning of this wonderful prayer. This book intends to open up the windows and allow heaven's light to fall upon this ancient prayer of our beloved Lord with the hope that you will be inspired—breathed upon by the Holy Spirit—and motivated to new dimensions of spiritual passion in your prayers.

We know The Lord's Prayer so well, but we know so little about it. We are sometimes guilty of Jesus' very words when He warns His disciples of meaningless repetitions. As we repeat this prayer over and over again we run the risk of the words falling into the abyss of hollow insignificance. The Lord's Prayer is rich in spiritual content and transcends our casual attempts at prayer in our times. John Reumann wrote these words in the introduction to the English translation of Joachim Jeremias' little book on The Lord's Prayer:

> Word for word, few creations in all the history of literature have received so much attention, and probably no other prayer has wielded as much influence in the history of religious devotions. In part this is because it is

the prayer, the only one, which the Lord of Christians, Jesus of Nazareth, enjoined on his disciples. Partly too, this prayer's unique position results from incessant usage, in church and without, and for our awareness that somehow we have never plumbed its depths.[2]

IF A LITTLE CHILD COMES, AWAKEN ME

There is a story told of Francis Xavier, who on one occasion was at the point of complete exhaustion. In giving direction to his servant, he exclaimed, "I must sleep, or I shall die. No matter who comes, do not disturb me. I must sleep." Hurrying to his tent, Xavier left his faithful servant to watch. In a little while, however, the servant saw Xavier's face return at the tent's door. His servant saw on his countenance a look of awe as though he had seen a vision. "I have made a mistake," Xavier said. "If a little child comes, awaken me."

Xavier knew the importance of God's Word. He must have remembered that in the Book of First Samuel, Eli the priest lay in his place when the child Samuel came calling. Xavier made it clear that he didn't want to miss out on a divine appointment of that magnitude if it were ever to arise. It is my desire to see the next generation come calling as well. You see, the Bible tells us that the word of the Lord was rare in Eli's days, and there was very little vision from God. Hence, can you possibly imagine how important Samuel, though a child, was to God? You see, God had found someone who could hear in Samuel. And, Eli was needed to bring clarity to this child. God chose to make a deposit in Samuel from which He would receive dividends at a later date. Therefore, if a little child comes, awaken me as well. I want to hear my Father's voice, and I want to know how to communicate with Him. Praying The Lord's Prayer is a step in that direction.

LORD, TEACH US TO PRAY

"It happened that while Jesus was praying in a certain place, after He had finished, one of His disciples said to Him, 'Lord, teach us to pray just as John also taught his disciples' " (Luke 11:1).

We are not sure which disciple made this request. It might have been Andrew, who was a disciple of John the Baptist before he left to follow Jesus. It was this personal request that occasioned the giving of The Lord's Prayer. In the times of Jesus, certain religious groups such as the Pharisees, the Essenes, and others had certain customs in prayer. This disciple of Jesus wanted to be instructed by his master in the spiritual art of prayer. It was probably the hope of the disciple that this prayer would identify and bind together this little group who were known as the followers of Jesus.

This simple request has been uttered thousands of times over the centuries as God's people have sought more meaningful and spiritual ways to pray. Tired of the ritualism associated with church prayers, they have longed to be free to touch heaven. Parched by the sun of religiosity in their spiritual exercises, they have endeavored to find ways to communicate with God in such a way that will lift them into new dimensions of spiritual fellowship with God.

Jesus would never turn down a request like this. He is attracted to such passionate and personal appeals on the part of His family. Looking deeply into the eyes of this disciple, He spoke to him and to the generations that would follow him. This prayer is His answer to the plea of all who have longed to know how to pray.

PRAY, THEN, IN THIS WAY

"Pray, then, in this way: 'Our Father is art in heaven, Hallowed be Your name" (Matt. 6:9).

In His introduction to The Lord's Prayer, Jesus instructs His disciples to pray in this manner or according to this pattern. The Master of prayer unlocks the door to His own private chambers and gives us a peek into how He prays and what matters most when one addresses the Father in prayer.

Thomas Watson (1620-1686) was one of the most popular preachers in London during the Puritan era. His writings are marked with clarity, raciness, and spiritual richness. His greatest contribution to our times is his work on The Lord's Prayer. Concerning this verse he wrote:

> "After this manner:" that is, let all your petitions agree and symbolize with the things contained in The Lord's Prayer; and well may we make all our prayers consonant and agreeable to this prayer. Tertullian calls it 'a breviary and compendium of the gospel,' it is like a heap of massive gold. The exactness of this prayer appears in the dignity of the Author. A piece of work has commendation from its artifices, and this prayer has commendation from its Author; it is The Lord's Prayer. As the moral law was written with the finger of God, so this prayer was dropped from the lips of the Son of God.[3]

This prayer is a key to the passions of Christ, giving clues to His zeal for His Father and His compassion for men. There are certain similarities between The Lord's Prayer and the Ten Commandments, for both address our relationship with God and our relationship with man.

Jesus is not indicating that we pray this prayer in some kind of mystical or rote way, which is simply using routine or repetition without complete comprehension. In fact, He sets this prayer in contrast to the way that the Jews and Gentiles pray:

When you pray, you are not to be like the hypocrites; for they love to stand and pray in the synagogues and on the street corners so that they may be seen by men. Truly I say to you, they have their reward in full. And when you are praying, do not use meaningless repetition as the Gentiles do, for they suppose that they will be heard for their many words (Matt. 6:5,7).

As His disciples pray in this manner they will avoid the traps of pious and "showbiz" praying that we often hear in church. He is leading them into the secret place to touch God in a way that they have never experienced before.

So the warning is clear from the beginning. Don't make this prayer like so many other prayers that become empty because they are not prayed with spiritual wisdom or fervor.

PARAPHRASE OF THE LORD'S PRAYER BY ST. FRANCIS OF ASSISI

St. Francis was well known for his prayer, "Lord, make me an instrument." St. Francis also regularly prayed The Lord's Prayer; here is his paraphrased rendition of it.

OUR FATHER
most holy,
our Creator and Redeemer,
our Saviour and our Comforter.

WHO ART IN HEAVEN
in the angels and the saints,
giving them light to know you,
since you, Lord, are light;
setting them afire to love you,
since you, Lord, are love;
dwelling in them

Adoratio

and giving them fullness of joy,
since you, Lord,
are the supreme, eternal good,
and all good comes from you.

HALLOWED BE THY NAME,
may we grow to know you better and better
and so appreciate the extent of your favors,
the scope of your promises,
the sublimity of your majesty,
and the profundity of your judgements.

THY KINGDOM COME,
so that you may reign in us by your grace,
and bring us to your kingdom,
where we shall see you clearly,
love you perfectly and,
happy in your company, enjoy you forever.

THY WILL BE DONE ON EARTH AS IT IS IN HEAVEN,
so that we may love you with all our heart,
by always having you in mind;
with all our soul
by always longing for you;
with all our mind,
by determining to seek your glory in everything;
and with all our strength,
of body and soul,
by lovingly serving you alone.
May we love our neighbors as ourselves,
and encourage them all to love you,
by bearing our share
in the joys and sorrows of others,

21

while giving offence to no one.

GIVE US THIS DAY OUR DAILY BREAD,
your beloved Son, our Lord Jesus Christ,
so that we may remember and appreciate
how much He loved us,
and everything he said and did and suffered.

AND FORGIVE US OUR TRESPASSES,
in your immeasurable mercy,
by virtue of the passion of your Son.

AS WE FORGIVE THOSE WHO TRESPASS AGAINST US,
and if we do not forgive perfectly,
Lord, make us forgive perfectly,
so that, for love of you,
we may really forgive our enemies,
and fervently pray to you for them,
returning no one evil for evil,
but trying to serve you in everyone.

AND LEAD US NOT INTO TEMPTATION,
be it hidden or obvious,
sudden or persistent.

BUT DELIVER US FROM EVIL,
past, present or future,

FOR THINE IS THE KINDOM AND THE GLORY FOREVER AND EVER.
Amen.[4]

It is my prayer that as you read this book, you will able to pray The Lord's Prayer with new meaning and greater zeal. I also pray that you will discover the world of success in God's kingdom in regards to praying prayer patterns. I also hope that you will be stimulated to lead and teach others to do the same. Many have.

CHAPTER ONE

Men Ought Always to Pray

The year was 1971, and GayNell, my wife of five years, and I had just moved back to Houston, Texas. We had returned to Texas in order to work as an assistant pastor to Hardie Weathers. Hardie was a great man of God who had, at that time, become the spiritual father figure in my life. Houston was experiencing a growth boom at that time in unprecedented measure. Thirty thousand people a month were moving into the greater Houston area. I believe Providence saw to it that we would be located in the East End of Houston during those days. The very location and the cross-cultural pollination of that specific area would be an education in itself, an education that nothing else could ever replace in our lives. The Goliath of prejudice would have to be faced in a battle that was being waged in the shadows of the city. There was a stand-off of indifference toward the growing needs of a drug-culture infested society. For the most part, the church had just simply turned its head and pretended that the problem was not there. I guess they thought that if they ignored it long enough it would go away.

The fast growth of the population made it almost impossible to hurry anywhere. There were no traffic loops to ease the congestion located throughout the city. What made matters worse was the fact that the city fathers did not have the forethought to build greatly needed bridges to get the ever-increasing traffic over railway intersections. You almost had to know the train schedule to get anywhere on time. Houston had become the largest city per square mile in the world. I could easily make nine hospital calls while traveling 150 miles in one day, without ever leaving the city limits.

It was during this season that my burden for ministry was truly born. I knew I had been called into the ministry. I had served as an assistant pastor to my uncle in a rural church in Stafford, Texas. GayNell and I had even served in pastoral ministry to one church located on the campus of Lamar University in Beaumont, Texas, and another located at the end of hundreds of miles of nothing in Uvalde, Texas. I would tell people in Uvalde that I was the pastor of the church in town; they would not believe me because they did not know the church was in town. It was not that Uvalde was so big; I think that at that time there was only one traffic light in the entire county. They were just unaware that it was around. GayNell and I laughed that it would have been good just for someone to stick their head in the door on a Sunday morning and shout, "Boo!"

ANOTHER LOVER ENTERS MY LIFE

Those first years were great. I was falling in love with another lover with whom my wife would have to share me for the rest of our lives. It was more than just an emotional attachment. My affection for her was evident to my wife. The other lover would take me away from my wife and family; my children would become jealous of her and even question, "Where is Daddy?" It was a precarious balance between my family and the other lover. We, of course, would have our differences but also times of intimacy and friendship. This lover would make demands that would require great blocks of time. I regret that I was too young to realize that some of the demands the other lover made on me were unreasonable. I just did not want to fail her any more than I would want to fail my wife. She deprived me of sleep and, over the years, to hear others tell it, she cost me my health to some degree. This is what one fellow told me when he said, "I make up the difference in what is lacking in my own body." In other words, if she did not use her gifts I would just have to give a little more effort and time myself. The cost was physical well-being.

What was even more difficult is this: She belonged to another. I remember the first time I realized I had fallen in love with her. It was a Sunday afternoon. A cool breeze blew across the bed through an open window where I was resting before I went back to spend a few hours with her. Have you ever told the Lord what you would or would not do? I have learned now that this is not necessarily the smartest thing a person can ever do. I knew of a man who told the Lord he would never go to a certain city, but by last accounts he died there some fifty years later. That afternoon I was giving the Lord my A-list of things that I would not be doing for Him, anytime in the near future or forever for that matter. Suddenly, His Word pierced my very being; the room was filled with His Word as much as it was filled with the breeze that blew through the window or the sunlight that lit up a room. His Word was as much in the room as I was; actually, it was more in the room than I was, and I was insignificant in regards to His Word that was filling the room. It was sharp and specific. It was more than someone quoting a Bible verse and then you giving mental consent to the fact that you had read it or even knew the passage. It came to me in first person, "I loved the Church and gave Myself for it." It was over—the love, His love, for another lover was sown into my heart like a seed in the earth.

For forty years my wife has shared me with this other lover, which I hope you have concluded by now is His Church. The love affair continues, and it is not just a calling, it is a shared life, a relationship that demands great respect. Some have a difficult time sharing their spouses with the family of God, only because they have not yet understood what I experienced that afternoon in a moment of encounter: "Christ loved the church and gave Himself for it."

When we moved back to Houston to work with the East End Church, the city had changed. Every third or fourth license plate was from another state. The war in Vietnam was the big national news, and it seemed the world was one big protest. Everyone was crying for entitlements, demanding some kind of power. The drug culture had not gone away as the church had hoped. It had not only swallowed up our end of the town, but it grabbed hold of some of the young people in the youth ministry of our church.

Unfortunately, I was locked into the religious box of what was expected of a young assistant pastor. Regardless of my surroundings, I was expected to be punctual and agreeable. One day I asked my pastor what I was to be called. "Am I your associate or your assistant?" His reply has never been forgotten. "What difference does it make?" Then he went on to say, "You abbreviate them both the same way." I still laugh at my youthful arrogance when I think about it. The pastor explained that he had seen titles ruin some good men. I guess that is what happens to those who become legends in their own mind.

There had been something of a historic restoration in the old Memorial Square in downtown Houston, which was only about three miles from where the church was located. A great number of tourists would often come to Allen's Landing looking for the local nightlife. Allen's Landing was rich with history, and local people knew it to be true. Two brothers named Allen ran a scam, selling acre lots of Houston to people in Chicago and New York City. They accomplished this feat by sending their carefully crafted sales posters to the adventurous and greedy out in these cities. Their posters showed Houston to be full of beautiful, cascading waterfalls with buffalo roaming in wide-open ranges when actually, the place was a swamp, and the only buffalo were the fish after which the local bayou was named.

WHEN A MOMENT BECOMES A MOVEMENT

One late Saturday night, we were driving home from a dinner engagement and we circled the Old Allen's Landing Memorial Square. We were in total amazement as we observed the thousands of people gathered there in a festive, "Mardi Gras" type atmosphere. People were honking the horns of their automobiles and hanging out of their car windows shouting at one another as though someone had just won a ball game. Young people were just hanging out, seemingly without purpose or direction. Many had packs on their backs looking for a place to crash for the night. We were left dumb and numb by this incredible sight. After some time, GayNell spoke up, breaking the silence. All she said was, "Somebody has to do something." When she said these words, it was like the voice of God pierced my heart. I still feel it to this day. For us, the next five years were defined by what originated in her heart that night. Little did we know that God's plan for our lives was a direct result of that one defining moment. My heart began to burn with a passion for the youth of my generation.

That *moment* became a *movement* in my life. I had to make a dramatic shift, moving away from a confining place of doing what was expected of me to a challenging place where I would do what I believe God wanted of me. A nomadic curse best describes where I was spiritually in my life before that day. The curse goes, "May you ever stand in one place." I was consumed with being good and, honestly, I was not very good at that. But, where would I begin?

I shared my concern with my pastor. He concluded that we must pray. As my father figure, he beautifully portrayed before me the example of a committed prayer life. I can still hear him say, "Some say that prayer is a duty. Prayer is not a duty. Prayer is a delight." His plan was that he and I would each take our turn going to church to pray every other morning. He announced to the church that we would be there, and if they had prayer requests they could call them in and we would pray over them daily. In the meantime, we were also praying that God would show us what to do in regards to an outreach into the community—a community that was changing from an upper middle-class neighborhood to basically one of rental properties. Many were moving to the suburbs to escape the changing times. Of course, we all know that we only take our problems with us. The lives of their children remained problematic as well. With this outflow of people leaving the city, we were left to deal with all the problems and prospects of a newly born inner city of Houston.

Praying the Kingdom Prayer

What I did not know was that, during this time, my pastor was secretly just teaching me how to pray. We began to pray, "Thy kingdom come in the East End of Houston as it is in

30

heaven." Nobody knew what we were praying about. It was top-secret, so to speak. I am not sure that we even knew what we were praying about, but God did. He had set our hearts to praying. At the end of the week, my pastor had a visit from an old friend who had known him as a young man. They lived in the same town many years before, and occasionally she would visit the church. She was moving to live with her daughter and son-in-law in another town and wanted to tell her old friend, my pastor, good-bye. The lady was twenty years or so his senior and God had been very good to her in life. I remember my pastor had great respect for her as a Christian. When he spoke of her, he spoke of her with dignity. I thought, "What a way to be known by others."

The lady was a spiritually-minded woman, and the Lord had told her to give her home (which consisted of a large house, a garage apartment situated above three garages, and a duplex) to the church. However, she had one stipulation. It must be used to work with the youth in the area. What was so wonderful about all this was *the timing* of her gift. It was the very thing for which we were praying! God heard us pray, "Thy kingdom come in the East End of Houston as it is in heaven." Through her obedience to the Father and her act of love, Mrs. Jamison opened the door to a divine experience of God's purposes and presence in our lives. These things would shape us for the remainder of a lifetime.

"Thy kingdom come, Thy will be done, on earth as it is in heaven," jumped off the pages of the Bible and into our hearts. These words were not casually spoken from our lips. They absolutely were not religious rhetoric. With that prayer on our lips, we entered into an extraordinary life full of adventure, as the Lord began to use us to establish His kingdom in many different countries of the world.

Within a few weeks of receiving the woman's exorbitant gift, a ministry was formed and began to function. Young people came to what we called Salt Inn Ministries. It was located on the corner of Brady and Marsden Streets, one block off Canal Street in the East End. It was as though we could feel a divine guidance that we had never experienced before. Each day, we could sense the hand of God leading us to pursue His will for our lives. We were marching to the tune of a different drummer.

Then, one day we took a short cut by Jackson Junior High School as we headed toward church on a Sunday afternoon. Driving by a tall chain fence that surrounded the playing field, I noticed that the school looked so dark. I prayed a simple prayer, "Oh God, give me that school." To my surprise, God spoke to me immediately. Deep down in my spirit, I heard him say, "Son, I *have* given you that school." I turned and told my wife what had just happened. I said, "GayNell, God just spoke to me and said, "Son, I have given you that school." She did not bat an eye. She was on God's side in that situation. I was outnumbered and there was no place to run. She said, "Well, I guess you had better get busy then." It was as though I was too naïve to know that I was "not supposed to" believe for something as great as that.

PRAYER – THE FIRE OF DESIRE

I have learned over the years that there are different types of prayer and, occasionally, we each find ourselves praying differently about certain things in our lives. It helped me when I discovered that there are some nineteen different words in Hebrew and Greek that show the believer the different aspects of prayer. Prayer takes many forms as the words flow from our spirit towards heaven's gates.

Luke 11:1 says, "It happened that while Jesus was pray-ing." The word for prayer here is a Greek word, *proseuchomai*. This word is highly suggestive, implying that Jesus was praying with fervency and intensity. F.E. Marsh, speaking of the ac-counts of prayer in the Book of Acts, said that, "Behind all these instances of prayer is the *fire of desire* which *moved* those who were found in the act of prayer." Jesus touched God's heart with His prayers, and he taught His apostles how to do the same. Our prayers must be prayed with fire. E.M. Bounds put it this way, "It takes heat, and fervency and meteoric fire, to push through, to the upper heavens, where God dwells with His saints, in light."[1]

James, the brother of Jesus, described in his book how Elijah was praying on Mt. Carmel, writing that Elijah was pleading with God that it would not rain. His prayer led God to put a stranglehold on the economy of a whole nation. Based upon that kind of praying James recorded, "The effec-tive prayer of a righteous man can accomplish much" (James 5:16). The white-hot prayer of a righteous man will prevail every time. Yearning for results like Jesus and the godly men of old, Jesus' disciples were hungry enough to ask Him to teach them to pray like He prayed. They had seen the passion and the power of His prayers, and they longed for that expe-rience in their own lives.

PRAYING AS JESUS PRAYED

"In the days of His flesh, He offered up both prayers and supplications with loud crying and tears to the One able to save Him from death, and He was heard because of His piety" (Heb. 5:7).

These words from the Book of Hebrews indicate the force with which Jesus prayed. The Greek words used in this passage, *ischuros* and *krauge*, indicate that Jesus offered His prayer with a strong and mighty outcry, an uproar of holy prayer. He was forceful, passionate, and powerful in His praying. His compelling and compassionate prayer was offered with a teardrop, as one commentator said.

There is something riveting in the prayers of Jesus that grips our hearts and urges us to pray in similar fashion. Our prayers should be marked with the same kind of urgency. They should never be limited to simply parroting memorized prayers, or monotonously reading words from a prayer book. In the words of our Master, they should not be "meaningless repetitions." Our prayers should be like those prayed by the early church as they interceded on behalf of Peter and John when they were locked up in the fourth ward of the prison. The power of their prayers shook heaven—and in return, heaven responded by shaking the earth. That night an earthquake rocked the old jailhouse and set the prisoners free. Let the Father come with His fullness into your life and through your fervent prayer so that He might rock your situation as well.

When we engage ourselves in prayer, we must allow ourselves to feel the urgency of the moment as we let our spirit connect with heaven. In that collision between heaven and earth, as man's spirit touches God's Spirit, holy passion is born, powerful prayers are spoken, and God's will is done.

PRAYER IN THE LIFE OF JESUS

Before you can understand the meaning of The Lord's Prayer, you have to understand the habit of the Lord as He gave Himself to prayer. Prayer was His life! It was not an addendum or an afterthought to His ministry. It was not what He did when all else failed or as something He turned to only in a time of crisis. Prayer was His strength, His joy, His very breath. Jesus began His public ministry in prayer, sustained it in prayer, modeled it in prayer, finished it in prayer, and now sits at the right hand of the Father, still praying for His own.

S.D. Gordon best described the importance of prayer in the life of Jesus with these words from his classic, *Quiet Talks on Prayer*:

> When God would win back His prodigal world He sent down a Man. That Man while more than man insisted upon being truly a man. He touched human life at every point. No man seems to have understood prayer, and to have prayed, as did He. How can we better conclude these quiet talks on prayer than by gathering about His person and studying His habits of prayer?
>
> A habit is an act repeated so often as to be done involuntarily; that is, without a new decision of the mind each time it is done.
>
> Jesus prayed. He loved to pray. Sometimes praying was His way of resting. He prayed so much and so often that it became a part of His life. It became to Him like breathing—involuntary.[2]

In the Gospels we get a clear picture of the praying Jesus. Fifteen different times the Gospel writers talk about His retreat to prayer.

> *But Jesus Himself would often slip away to the wilderness and pray* (Luke 5:16).

> *It was at this time that He went off to the mountain to pray, and He spent the whole night in prayer to God* (Luke 6:12).

PRAYING THE LORD'S PRAYER

Some eight days after these sayings, He took along Peter and John and James, and went up on the mountain to pray (Luke 9:28).

Jesus was not just a teacher of prayer. He prayed. His life modeled what He taught. It was this passion for prayer in the life of Jesus that motivated the disciples to ask Jesus to teach them to pray. Jesus provides the passion and the pattern for all those who would learn to pray in a way that will open heaven's door. It is called *The Lord's Prayer.*

CHAPTER TWO

The Power of Prayer

I have always prayed, but I have not always prayed powerfully. My prayer life changed forever after the week that I alternated praying daily in the church with our pastor. A solid resolve was formed in my life during that time. Prayer was becoming a vital part of my spiritual life. I began to see its effects in every other area of my life, including the life of my family. God graciously answered many prayers. He continued to lead us in ministry, and He incessantly blessed us because of His goodness toward us. His benefits even before that time could never be discounted, but that week marked a change in our ministry on behalf of the Kingdom.

When I think of the things that we prayed for, the things that we agonized over, I am reminded of the prayer of Hannah, the mother of Samuel. When she prayed for a son, she prayed unselfishly, disinterested in her own gain. She wanted a son that she could offer to her God.

It is hard to imagine a person actually praying with the purpose of God in mind. If God would give her a son, she would give the son back to Him. The die was cast. The prayer was prayed, and the answer came. She got what she requested, and, in return, God got what He desired. A closer look at her prayer life is very revealing. In First Samuel Chapter 1, we find that Hannah was in bitterness of soul, which means she was discontented and depressed. She was focused and consumed with her prayers, and no amount of consolation could satisfy her. The Hebrew word for her prayer is *palal*, which means "to judge self and to pray habitually." It is often used in the Old Testament, and it references the act of prayer. Her prayer was not a casual prayer. She was fanatical and, like Jacob of old, she wrestled with God to get His response.

In this type of prayer, it is as if your thoughts are like a Rubik's Cube, and you keep turning them until all sides match. This is what Hannah did, and uncompromising was the determination she had. She did not let go until God finally answered. She got her son and God got His prophet.

S.D. Gordon said that prayer must have two parts.

First, a God to give. "Yes," you say, "certainly, a God wealthy, willing, all of that." And, just as certainly, there must be a second factor, a man to receive. Man's willingness is God's channel to the earth. God never crowds nor coerces. Everything God does for man and through man He does with man's consent, always. With due reverence, but very plainly, let it be said that God can do nothing for the man with shut hand and shut life. There must be an open hand and heart and life through which God can give what He longs to. An open life, an open hand, open upward, is the pipeline of communication between the heart of God and this poor, old world. Our prayer is God's opportunity to get into the world that would shut Him out.[1]

AND SO I PRAYED...

I did not know exactly what God wanted each time I prayed. I simply knew I had to pray until His needs were satisfied. We were sort of like Nehemiah when the king asked him why he was looking so sad. Nehemiah had received word from Jerusalem concerning the plight of his people because of the devastation of the walls around the city. His heart had been heavy ever since he had received the word. Now an opportunity had presented itself. When he told the king the reason for his sadness, the king asked him what he wanted. How should he respond? The Bible says, "So I prayed to the God of heaven" (Neh. 2:4). Prayer is the proper response as opportunity knocks on our door.

During those days we continually prayed, and we fasted for the youth of Houston. Our hearts were being turned towards the plight of these precious young people whose lives had been devastated by the curse of drugs and alcohol. God answered and gave us clear direction. As we prayed, our hearts were being changed, preparing us to accept God's answer when it did come.

The only way I can describe what happened is this: It was as if we were sitting at a railroad crossing, watching the cars creep to a stop. As the conductor gets to where he wants the locomotive to be, he reverses the engines to bring the train to a halt. However, the momentum of the loaded down boxcars continues in its forward motion. As he struggles to reverse the process, the cars farther down the long line of connected cars continue rolling, ever so slowly. As you watch, you can see that even though he has stopped the forward motion, they still inflexibly progress in the same old direction. The noise of the coupling hitches crashing together in a hundred cars or more make for an enormously loud collision.

We were cruising along praying our prayers, and when the answer came it was hard to stop and just say 'yes' to the answered prayer. God put us in a place where, even though we prayed for Him to lead us and have His way in our lives, it was shallow at best. We had no clue what God was up to. God has a way of getting what He wants. He lets you pray yourself into a corner, and then He lets you see what you have done. We became the answer to our own prayers. It was as though a dream was being conceived in our hearts while we were praying. Prayer has an amazing power. While you are focused on your prayers, God is focused on your hearts. I don't know how many times my heart has changed while I was in the place of prayer. As we are trying to get our way, God is getting His way. What an amazing God we serve!

> The Holy Ghost comes down into our hearts sometimes in prayer with a beam from heaven, whereby we see more at once of God and His glory, more astounding thoughts and enlarged apprehensions of God, many beams meeting in one and falling to the center of our hearts. By these coming downs or divine influxes, God slides into our hearts by beams of Himself. We come not to have communion with God by way of many broken thoughts put together, but there is a contraction of many beams from heaven, which is shed into our souls. So that we know more of God, and have more communion with Him in a quarter hour than we could know in a year by the way of wisdom alone.[2]

These events were the beginning of the autobiography of my prayer life as I was learning to use The Lord's Prayer as a pattern for praying. During those times of prayer He also graciously shined His light on a box we were to step outside of.

THE VELVET BRICK

We were quite unaware that we were living our Christian life in a box. I can honestly say I had no clue that the box even existed in my ministry, let alone that I was stuck in it. I was like a pet goldfish a man had. Yes, he loved and appreciated that fish. Fed it. Cared for it. And yet, he kept it in a glass bowl. The fish existed, but it had no freedom. I lived in the fishbowl of what was expected of me for so long that I did not realize how it was robbing me *daily* of my destiny. Most of us have lived in that box, that fishbowl. We are controlled by our own expectations and the expectations of others. We have sought security over sacrifice.

Oh, how "secure" I was! Nice wife, nice apartment, nice furniture. Nice people around me, nice family, nice income. Nice church to be a part of...I had become the essence of "nice." Nevertheless, *nice* was not a fruit of the Spirit. Never has been, never will be! It was high time for me to experience what they call in the Bible Belt of America "The Velvet Brick." My status quo was about to be greatly challenged.

We must all learn the gospel that works *outside* the walls of the church as well. In fact, the gospel is for those who live on the other side of the street and have not experienced the radical nature of Father's love. They have experienced the judgmental spirit of too many Christians, but they are rather unfamiliar with the warmth of the Father's mercy.

I remember one man sharing with me as he was remorse-fully looking back over his life. He told me he knew how, all his life, he had performed what was expected of him. But it was a service without passion or compassion. He never felt the Father's love for the ones he ministered to. Regret was eating him up, and the reproach of his actions had seeped down into his bones. He was left with nothing but a memory and a doctrine. The truth about doctrine is that you can be 100 percent correct in doctrine and 100 percent wrong in relationship. The fact is that man's doctrine never moves people. Truth that is not laced with tenderness is empty and hollow, for both the speaker and the receiver.

I asked an elderly minister to give one word of advice to a group of ten or twelve young ministers lunching with us one day. I will never forget his exceptional words, "If I *would* have, I *could* have done more."

A man loved his goldfish and wanted to expand the world of his little friend. So, he filled up his bathtub with water and heated it to just the right temperature. Carefully, he took his little friend out of the fishbowl and placed him in the tub. To his surprise, the fish only swam around in an area that equaled the dimension of his fishbowl he had become familiar with. I was like that fish whom God had placed in a larger part of His world—a brand new world created by prayer. It was a world that He extravagantly loved and His Son had selflessly died for. It was a world that was right at our doorstep and we hardly ever noticed.

I am absolutely amazed when I consider what it took for God to introduce me to His world. It happened when I started praying, "Thy kingdom come, Thy will be done in the East End of Houston as it is in heaven." The Holy Spirit skillfully deposited that prayer in my heart and seared it on my lips. As I prayed, God would decisively answer in a way beyond my imagination.

> Behind the prayer of faith stand forces unimaginable.
> The prophet's servant watched with wondering awe the shining cohorts ride
> He who prays in faith raises his eyes beyond earth's highest hill,
> Snaps to the link, turns the frail switch to find
> Range upon range stand marshaled all the forces of the

THE POWER OF PRAYER

skies:
Out to their farthest bounds the message thrills.
And to his aid the legions twelve (by Christ refused)
In mighty rank on rank close up behind.
Then shout for him the morning spheres! The morning
stars.
And those etheric, all-embracing Powers
Which mock man's greatest might join in the cry:
"If God be for him who can be against him?
He has called on his maker! To his aid we fly!"

Author Unknown

PRAYERS ACCORDING TO GOD'S DESIRES

Real prayer is something God puts in your heart as a *desire* first. The psalmist David was a man of prayer, and the Psalms are full of little keys and insights into the life of prayer. "Delight yourself in the Lord; and He will give you the desires of your heart" (Ps. 37:4). I read this a bit differently from what some modern theologians and preachers teach. When I truly delight myself in the Lord, the desires that begin to form in my spirit are a gift from God. When I prayed for His Kingdom to come, He gave me His desires. Want a litmus test of where your desires lie? Examine the words of your prayers. Are you more consumed with your own personal wishes or for the world around you? In my situation, the answer to that question was forming in my spirit. I had become gripped by the grace of God that was reaching out to young people on the streets.

The answers to our prayers did not come without struggle! I remember the times when our money was low and we ran out of gas, those times being often, and the young people would have to push us to the gas station. Some would not even ride with us, because we drove an old Lincoln at that time and

43

they thought it looked like a character car. They were afraid they would get arrested if they were caught with us, if for nothing else other than suspicion.

I remember the day I went to stake a spiritual claim on the property of the school for which I was deeply burdened. I asked the principle if I could conduct an assembly with the student body. God had prepared his heart even though he was a professed agnostic at that time. To my surprise and probably his, he agreed. However, he said we could only have a thirty minute session. I demanded an hour. I am sure he anticipated the worst-case scenario. We brought in a Christian band from California that just happened to be traveling through our area. The band included guitars and drums, and they sang songs that the young people could understand. A message of God's love was being communicated to them.

It happened in a flash! A young girl came running down to the front of the platform. No invitation had been given, but she was hurting. Her story eventually unfolded. She had been violated and taken advantage of, leaving her with a shame she did not understand nor with which she could cope. I will never forget what she said, "Mister, can you help me? My grandmother (who was her legal guardian) says I have conviction, and that is what makes me so mean." *Right then and there His kingdom came to this desperate young girl.* That was the moment of contact. Heaven had reached the heart of this young girl. Heaven's answer had started the journey a long time ago while we were praying but had manifested itself in our world right there in this troubled teen.

God broke through, and for the next forty-five days heaven came down into the hearts of young people in that inner-city public school in Houston, Texas. We had prayer every morning before class. The students and teachers met in the lunchroom and prayed earnestly for the student body. It was "in" to be a part of what was going on and "out" not to be. God hijacked the school for many reasons; most we would not understand until a few years later.

What happened in those days to us and through us was an absolute surprise. We were like those in the Book of Acts who prayed for the release of Peter and John. And yet, they needed faith that their prayers would avail. When Rhoda told the others Peter was standing outside (as a result of their prayers), they pretty much told her she had lost it. Peter had to keep on knocking to finally get in. Sometimes God's people are still praying when He has already answered their prayers. Prayer and faith must be linked together. E.M. Bounds, that master on prayer, said, "The possibilities of prayer are the possibilities of faith. Prayer and faith are Siamese twins. One heart animates them both. Faith, is always praying. Prayer, is always believing. Faith must have a tongue by which it can speak. Prayer is the tongue of faith."[3]

We have no way of knowing how many came to Christ in those outreaches, but the results of this invasion from heaven continue to bear fruit over thirty years later.

I was back in Houston for some special services a couple of years ago, and a beautiful young Hispanic girl came up to me and said, "You don't know me, but I know you." She was one of the spoils of war waged in the East End of Houston in 1971-1976. This precious girl went on to tell me that she was the granddaughter of an old friend we ministered to in Zavala Park. He was a notorious addict, even by the standards on the streets.

Her life had been changed during those days. She now loved God and was clean. Because of God's kingdom coming years before, this girl was raised to serve God. Her story made my day! I honestly don't remember how the service went that night. I was simply looking into the face of an old dream I had dreamed over thirty years ago. Santos, one of the incredible young men we had taken into our lives in that time, had brought her to the meeting. Our Santos, working as a drug counselor in one of the schools we had ministered in thirty years before.

Prayer releases God's kingdom, but first it is planted as a seed in our own hearts. Origen, one of the great fathers of the Church, said that he who prays for the coming of God's kingdom prays rightly to have it within himself, that there it may grow and bear fruit and become perfect. As the Kingdom grows within us, it will then be manifested and released in all that we do.

If you allow God to work *in* you and *through* you, if you hang on to *His desires* rather than your own, His Kingdom will just keep coming in your life as well.

CHAPTER THREE

Our Father

ather—just the mention of that word can create a warm sense of security and acceptance or, on the other hand, it can generate feelings of anger and rejection. It all depends upon the hearer. Jesus' own word for God is *Father*. It occurs twelve times in the Sermon on the Mount, and more than a hundred times in St. John's Gospel. One must never confuse our concepts of *Father* with the way Jesus used it. Jesus elevates the word out of its human perceptions and places it on the high mountains of heavenly reality. It is important for us to understand that Jesus was not just looking for a word that would help man to interpret God. He was not searching for an anthropological model in which to explain the unexplainable Almighty. The word *Father*, in its most sublime and noble sense, is the essence of who God is. It is intrinsic to His nature and unique to His relationship with the creation. Out of His Father-heart mankind was birthed. He was, is, and always shall be initiator, creator, protector, lover, provider, sustainer, and the beginning and end of all things. He is the Father of all mankind.

> Nay, the fatherhood which Scripture predicates of God is not something which God is like, but something which He essentially is. The really startling fact is this, that instead of the living fatherhood being a reflection of human fatherhood, it is human fatherhood which is an intended reflection of the divine![1]

It is widely known that the attributes of His Fatherhood are often mentioned in the Old Testament references to God. His tender mercies are revealed in scriptures such as, " Just as a father has compassion on his children, so the Lord has compassion on those who fear Him" (Ps. 103:13). Or, "But now, O Lord, You are our Father, we are the clay, and You our potter; and all of us are the work of Your hand"(Isa. 64:8).

> The new meaning that Christ poured into the word, 'Father', was that, God is the Father as well as the Creator of the individual. Christ said that He came to reveal the Father, and this was an important part of His revelation of God, that God is our Father. The mystery, the power, the goodness of God is summed up in that name which He always used in speaking of Him, 'Father'.[2]

ABBA, OUR FATHER

> *One time Jesus was somewhere praying, when he stopped, one of his followers said to Him, "John taught his followers how to pray, Lord, please teach us how to pray, too." Jesus said to them, "When you pray, pray like this:* **Father, may Your kingdom come.***'"* (Luke 11:2).[3]

The use of the word *Father* in the Old Testament is rather rare. Only on fourteen occasions is the word used. The use of the word *Father* in the Old Testament reaches its highest worth in the writings of the prophets.

"Then I said, 'How I would set you among My sons and give you a pleasant land, the most beautiful inheritance of the nations!' And I said, 'You shall call Me, My Father, and not turn away from following Me'" (Jer. 3:19).

"'Is Ephraim My dear son? Is he a delightful child? Indeed, as often as I have spoken against him, I certainly still remember him; therefore My heart yearns for him; I will surely have mercy on him,' declares the Lord" (Jer. 31:20).

Through the voice of Jeremiah, the Father-heart of God is revealed. The echo of these words reverberates clearly in our own time, assuring us of the Father's mercy and compassion. Can there be any deeper demonstration of the meaning of the word *Father* than what is penned by the ancient prophet?

Jesus picks up on this theme that seems to have been lost in the Jewish culture. He drives it home in more dramatic fashion by His use of the word *Abba*. Chrysostom, the early church father, said that in the Aramaic, *Abba* was how a small child addressed his father, equivalent to our word *Daddy*. The Talmud confirms this when it says: "When a child experiences the taste of wheat, it learns to say abba and imma (dear father and dear mother)."[4] *Abba* and *imma* are the first sounds that a young child stammers. No Jew had ever dared to address God in this way. The Catholic theologian, Joaquim Jeremias, said that, with the help of his staff, he examined all of the prayer literature of late Judaism and that there was no place in this immense literature that referred to God as Abba.

Not only did Jesus use the word *Father* when addressing God, He also taught His disciples to do so as well. In the Sermon

PRAYING THE LORD'S PRAYER

on the Mount, Jesus repeatedly used the term *Father* when teaching his disciples about prayer:

> *But you, when you pray, go into your inner room, close your door and pray to your Father who is in secret, and your Father who sees what is done in secret will reward you* (Matt. 6:6).

> *So do not be like them; for your Father knows what you need before you ask Him* (Matt. 6:8).

> *Pray, then, in this way: "Our Father who is in heaven, hallowed be Your name"* (Matt. 6:9).

> *For if you forgive others for their transgressions, your heavenly Father will also forgive you* (Matt. 6:14).

> *Look at the birds of the air, that they do not sow, neither do they reap nor gather into barns, and yet your heavenly Father feeds them. Are you not worth much more than they?* (Matt. 6:26).

> *For the Gentiles eagerly seek all these things; for your heavenly Father knows that you need all these things* (Matt. 6:32).

By this exhortation Jesus draws his disciples into the intimacy of the relationship with His Father. As He is a Son, they too are sons of the Father. He longs for them to transcend a relationship with God that is based upon religious exercises. He woos them into the secret place that He has discovered and teaches them how to sit on the lap of the Father. In that secret place their prayers will be transformed into reality, and the dreams of their heart will find expressions on the earth.

GOD'S WORLD BECOMES MY WORLD

From the time started praying, "Thy kingdom come, Thy will be done," God's world became my world. My world, up until that time, was quite small, but now I was being stretched as God took me into a world I did not know. One certainly could not pray that prayer and remain content living in a religious culture with racial prejudice. If He were my Father then He was also the Father of others. I was being pressured to bring others into the family of God.

There were times when I was called upon to administer last rites to Catholics, and there were also times when I would speak in schools and counsel drug addicts who knew more of the Scripture than I did. I worked day and night with the "up and outers" and the "down and outers," only to discover that their problems were all the same. Though there was much lip service, many had never really come into a Father/son relationship with God. They had not experienced the mercy of their heavenly Father, nor had they heard His words of redemption and healing.

As we prayed over and over again, calling out to "Our Father," all barriers began to come down, racial and religious. Though the racial barrier was never a major issue in my life, I found that when we prayed to "Our Father," a new understanding of His love for all men was being birthed in my heart. Many young Hispanic youth had quickly become a part of our extended family. The loudest and most conspicuous was a teenager named Jacob Aranza. We would always laugh when people would ask who Jacob's parents were and he would say that GayNell and I were his parents. Our kinship turned a few heads, but the sacrifice was well worth the reward.

PRAYING THE LORD'S PRAYER

LORD, TEACH ME TO PRAY

It was a damp rainy Wednesday night in Houston, and we were at church as usual. For some time I had been calling out to the Lord to teach me how to pray. He answered my requests by sort of trapping me in a predicament that taught me a great deal about the Father and my prayers. If you ask Him to teach you to pray, He will willingly put you into situations where *you will have to pray.*

On this Wednesday night, I was called out of the service to go to the Harris County Jail to get one of the church family's sons out of jail for public intoxication. I had just gone out the side door when I saw a commotion in the front of the church building. Hurrying up to a small crowd of ushers standing in front of the building, I saw that one of our family's brand new cars had been rear-ended by another car. The driver had been taken in to the vestibule of the church to see if he was okay, only to find out he was dead drunk. On top of that, he could not speak English. I yelled out, "Call the police!" Since *police* sounds very much like the Spanish translation, *policia*, the man immediately took off, running down the street. This guy did not want any encounter with the law. I took off after him. Unfortunately, no one followed him but me. I looked back again in desperation, but not one brave foot soldier was following with me in the chase.

The Spanish man ran for about a block and a half as I steadfastly pursued him. Suddenly, he stopped; huffing and puffing, I was glad for a short break. Bad news! He had only stopped to pull out a knife. Flashing the knife, it was clear that he had every intention of attacking me if I came any closer. I simply pulled off my raincoat, wrapping it around my arm for protection from him and his weapon. My breath was thick, as time was held suspended for what seemed an eternity. What I

52

did not realize was that heaven had set me up. God is like that, you know.

The man, heeding my gesture, turned and began to scramble off again. This time, he wildly fled into a back hallway of a lounge and pool hall located on Harrisburg Street, which was a couple of blocks away from the church. Within minutes, nine police cars showed up. In retrospect, the event felt like I was on a "Bad Boys" television segment of *Cops*.

The police invaded the building, scurrying like ants on a molehill, only to come out sometime later with no one in custody. Abruptly, they admonished me, "You come and help us look." I knew this wasn't protocol, and my better judgment suggested I should not go, but I went anyway. We went up the stairs into the cheap apartments above the pool hall with the lounge below. The music blared from a distant jukebox, breaking the silence of the night as we walked down a hallway. One light bulb dangled from an exposed wire hanging from a high ceiling. The police opened the first door as they commanded me to stand back. Heeding their instructions was no problem on my part. With guns drawn, they shined their flashlights into a dark room only to see a naked man, totally emaciated, lying in his own waste on a bare, cold floor. I don't know to this day if he was dead or alive, and those with me were not the least bit concerned. To this day I still remember the horrible smell emanating from his body. I told the officers that this was not the room, and we moved on down the dimly lit hallway to an apartment door located at the end of the hall.

They knocked on the door, and a frightened wife with several small children opened the door. A Spanish-speaking officer turned to me and asked, "What do you think?" I said, "This is where he is." They found him hiding in a closet and arrested him for the accident right in front of his children.

The police left me alone in the hallway, and I was heartsick at what had just taken place. I felt no satisfaction in being a part of apprehending the man. The sight of this man's condition as his wife and kids fearfully looked on was troubling. Wearily, I leaned over against a wall with a sense of futility pounding in my head. As I turned to walk down the hall, God spoke to me, and the words I heard changed my life. I heard the voice of God saying, "Son, it is one thing to go *to* the world and another to go *into* all the world." My tears were dry, but I wept. I decided to go make bail for the young man in jail. On the way I had plenty to think about. The *into* God wanted me to find was just two blocks from the church. It wasn't in the jungles of Africa. It was just down the street. For the fellow in jail, I was an answer to prayer. But, I realized I had so much to learn about this world. I never understood how much pain and agony there was in the world of man.

PRAYING LIKE JESUS

I suppose the picture of a spoiled child crawling up in his father's lap going through his pockets *to get from him what he wants* is a poor illustration of what it means to pray, "Our Father." But that is how most of us pray. Up until that point it was a pretty good picture of what my prayer life had been like. It would take me years to learn and continue to learn that the prayers God answers are those Jesus spoke of in John 14:13, "Whatever you ask in My name, that will I do, so that the Father may be glorified in the Son."

The purpose of prayer is to glorify God and to align us with His purposes. The scales were falling off my eyes, like Hallesby says in his book, Prayer. In new ways I was seeing the misuse of prayer and the difficulties connected with prayer.

> *Prayer life has its own laws, as all the rest of life has. The fundamental law in prayer is this: Prayer is given and ordained*

for the purpose of glorifying God. Prayer is the way appointed of giving Jesus an opportunity to exercise His supernatural powers of salvation. And in so doing, He desires to make use of us.[5]

We must learn to let Him have his way in us. Prayer is more than just talking about things. There is a spiritual dynamic that takes place in the process of prayer. We are engaging Father in such a way that, as we pray, something is happening in us. Through prayer we enter the realm where Father lives. We step out of our world into His world—the world of the Spirit. As we live in that world, we begin to see things differently in our world.

NEVER PRAY WHEN YOU ARE HIDING FROM THE FATHER

Norman Vincent Peale spoke of a boyhood incident in his life. In his story, he tells us of how he got hold of a big, black cigar and headed into a back alley where no one would see him. He lit it, and it didn't taste good. Nevertheless, smoking it made him feel grown up. Amidst his defiant puffs, he saw his father coming. Norman quickly put the cigar behind his back and tried to act as casual as possible. He and his father exchanged pleasantries for a moment, and then, trying to divert his father's attention in any way possible, Norman came up with an idea after having spied a billboard advertising the circus. "Can I go, Dad?" he pleaded. "Can I go to the circus when it comes to town? Please, Dad?" His father's reply was one that Norman never forgot. It is one we would do well to remember as well.

"Son," his father answered quietly but firmly. "One of the first lessons you need to learn about life is this: Never make a petition while at the same time trying to hide a smoldering disobedience behind your back."[6]

TALKING TO THE FATHER

When you think of who a father is in the finest sense of the word, there are many things that should encourage you. When you approach God in prayer, you should come to Him with high expectations of Him as your Heavenly Father—it is to this loving Father we are to make our requests known. He stands ready to provide for you and invites you to ask of Him. When you ask from your place of need, He hears you and answers accordingly.

> *Or what man is there among you who, when his son asks for a loaf, will give him a stone? Or if he asks for a fish, he will not give him a snake, will he? If you then, being evil, know how to give good gifts to your children, how much more will your Father who is in heaven give what is good to those who ask Him!* (Matt. 7:9-11).

He is prepared to listen and encourages us to call upon Him. I am not suggesting you pray slot machine prayers, throwing your prayers up to heaven hoping that one of them will hit the jackpot. Nor should you pray in a robotic manner, repetitiously asking God to answer you without knowing what you are speaking or believing that it will even come true. Jesus told His disciples not to pray empty phrases, which means He doesn't want us to just babble on endlessly. It is not a matter of the quantity of our prayers, but the quality and the passion of our hearts.

Jesus himself taught us to pray, "Our Father." We can repeat those words often and lovingly without them being mindless. When we say "Father" it should generate an immediate response of faith and trust in our hearts. We can come to the Father because we trust Him.

Therefore, we can pray with faith that He will hear us. He isn't like so many dads who, with their favorite sports programming blaring, don't hear a word their kids are saying. You can trust that He hears you, and you can have faith that He will respond from His father's heart.

The attitude of faith is important when you are talking to your Father. You see, prayers without faith are empty prayers. Appreciate that if your Father knows, then everything is going to work together for His good, and it will be good for you also. In my life, God worked not only *through* me but also *in* me as I surrendered my will to His supreme will for my life. That old drunk in that prison cell got blessed because I prayed, but my Father also did something in my heart. He was working according to the good pleasure of His will, even though there were days I felt like saying, "Are we having fun yet?" As my friend and psychologist, Terry Lyles, says, "Stress is good for you." I was learning that my prayers were not delivering me from my troubles but were giving me the strength to walk through my troubles. As a good Father, He was training me to be a son.

When my brother and I were children, my dad would measure us to see who was growing the most. He would stand us in the doorway of the kitchen and make a mark on the doorjamb to see how much we had grown. I would always cheat just a little because I wanted to be taller than my dad was. We would walk by weekly when he was not around just to see if we had grown anymore.

Well, that is the way it was with our prayer life. Father God made the mark on an old tree called calvary so that, from time to time, we can see how much we have grown. It is not for Him to see. He already knows the progress we are making. In the place of prayer and in the presence of the Father we are learning how to live our lives in such a manner so that men might see our good works and glorify our Father in heaven. Christ lived His life glorifying God the Father as well. He is our supreme example in how to live in relationship with the Father.

JESUS AND HIS FATHER

Jesus' devotion to the Father is fueled by the profound love affair that exists between Father and Son. It is clear that the Father deeply loves the Son. The Son has the full attention of the Father. Other things never distract Jesus. He is consistently in tune with the love the Father shows Him.

The Father loves the Son and has given all things into His hand (John 3:35).

For the Father loves the Son, and shows Him all things that He Himself is doing; and the Father will show Him greater works than these, so that you will marvel (John 5:20).

My friend Don Milam describes the Father's response to His Son's love in this way:

Because of that great love, the Father has placed the totality of His Divine, eternal purpose into the hands of the Son. He trusts the Son implicitly to carry out the desires of His heart. Father rests in His love and trust for the Son. Therefore, He pulls back the veil between the spirit realm and the physical, allowing the Son to see the work of the Father. To the deep gratification of the Father, the Son reciprocates with His own response of passionate love. The Son longs to perpetually live in the Presence of the Father, and He wholeheartedly commits Himself to the work of the Father.[7]

As one who understood the power of obedience to the will of the Father that He discovered in the place of prayer, Jesus tells His disicples that, "He who has My commandments and keeps them is the one who loves Me; and he who loves Me will be loved by My Father, and I will love him and will disclose Myself to him"

(John 14:21). He continues, "Just as the Father has loved Me, I have also loved you; abide in My love" (John 15:9).

What awesome words! Jesus invites the disciples to participate in the fellowship of that love. As He obeys the Father in all things, so too the disciples are invited to enter through the door of obedient submission to the will of the Father and into that circle of love.

When you resolve to take the plunge from the lofty peak of religious expectations, diving into the darkness that surrounds those who are lost and desperate in this world plagued by sin, you'll find it is like base-jumping off the side of a mountain. It is an exhilarating plunge that will cause you to cry out, "My Father!" I chose to take that plunge, and it was in those days that I began to address God in a more personal way, "My Father."

I am often imitated and accused of saying this frequently—"My Father." Now, it is almost an unconscious prayer, spoken from my lips in times of trouble or need. It is a prayer that may be the difference between life and death. As someone once said, it's between shining or showing off. My voice is raspy, always has been, but when my grandchildren drop their voices to imitate me, I have to admit it gives me a chuckle that they don't understand.

More than anything, I want them to get to know Him as Father, and I want you to know Him as Father in the desperate and decisive times in which we live. And...the sooner, the better.

CHAPTER FOUR

The Windows of Heaven

So that you may be sons of your Father who is in heaven; for He causes His sun to rise on the evil and the good, and sends rain on the righteous and the unrighteous (Matt. 5:45).

Beware of practicing your righteousness before men to be noticed by them; otherwise you have no reward with your Father who is in heaven (Matt. 6:1).

So that your giving will be in secret; and your Father who sees what is done in secret will reward you (Matt. 6:4).

But you, when you pray, go into your inner room, close your door and pray to your Father who is in secret, and your Father who sees what is done in secret will reward you (Matt. 6:6).

Not everyone who says to Me, 'Lord, Lord,' will enter the kingdom of heaven, but he who does the will of My Father who is in heaven will enter. (Matt. 7:21).

Heaven is the dwelling place of the Father, the location of His throne, the habitation for His presence. Every family must have a home, for their home is the center of their activities. It is the expression of who the family is in community. For our heavenly Father, heaven is His home.

Heaven is the center of the invisible realm in which God lives. Heaven is the place where the fullness of the Father's presence is manifested. Every divine activity on earth proceeds from heaven, but His presence is only in "testimony" here on the earth. To address God is to address Him in heaven: "Our Father who art in heaven." Heaven is His place of residence. It is the place where He is most comfortable, and it is filled with angelic worship and perfect harmony. Heaven is characterized by perfect rest and glorious symmetry.

Men are trying to get to heaven while God is trying to get heaven to men. It is the will of the Father to relate everything on earth to heaven. "Thy kingdom come. Thy will be done, on earth as it is in heaven." The Son comes as the full expression of heaven, representing heaven in its fullest import. *He comes to establish heaven's rule in the affairs of man.*

> The Bible teaches us that God is located in heaven. 'God is in heaven,' (Ecclesiastes 5:2): that is the declaration. It teaches that there is a system, an order, in heaven, which is the true one and which is the ultimate one. In the end, it will be the reproduction of a heavenly order upon this earth which will be the consummation of all the counsels of God. Christ came down from heaven and returned to heaven.[1]

BECOMING A PRAYER

Do you remember how Daniel prayed and, as a result, Gabriel came to see him with a message from God? "So I gave my attention to the Lord God to seek Him by prayer and supplications, with fasting, sackcloth and ashes" (Dan. 9:3). The Hebrew word used for prayer here is *Tephillah*, which means "to make individual supplication." When the psalmist made supplications of God, saying, "Hear my prayer," the same word was used. There are times we pray corporately, but more often, we pray individually.

Great men of old sought God in this manner as well. *Tephillah* is the word of choice for the way David, Moses, Solomon, Daniel, Manasseh, Nehemiah, Job, the prophet Habbakuk, and others defined their disposition in prayer. David used this word in Psalm 109: 4 when he sang, "**I AM PRAYER.**" If David had a hi-liter at his disposal, I'm sure he would have used it on this verse. As a majestic leader of others, David learned it is one thing to pray, and entirely another thing to *become* a prayer.

As my team and I were growing up in the ministry, heaven became very real to us, and we often found ourselves in situations where we were desperate for help from heaven. We understood where our real help would come from. "My help comes from the Lord, who made heaven and earth" (Ps. 121:2).

GETTING HELP FROM HEAVEN

Here is a story that was repeated many times on the streets of Houston in those days. I remember the day when an addict was going to break into the Salt Inn with the intention of burglarizing the place, hoping he could get electronic equipment that he could pawn quickly. You see, he needed fast cash for a quick fix. We had a couple who lived in an apartment in what we called the Big White House. Dale and Barbara were incredible people, and they were known to share everything they had with the young people from the street. We could not have done the work God asked us to do by ourselves, and we were delighted to have these ministers by our side. They were genuine pastors to these young people in a true New Testament sense of the word.

Both of them worked on secular jobs, so the facility was not protected in the daytime hours. The thief in question had cased the place, deciding to go up the back steps to break through the kitchen door. As he began to move toward the house, however, a large man suddenly appeared out of nowhere and stood on the steps. There were no bushes or cars nearby. And there was certainly no place the man could have come from to position himself in front of the culprit. He simply appeared, and the thief disappeared.

It is said the man glowed. Our help had come from heaven, and from that day on—as long as we worked in the house—there was never another incident like that in our ministry. Heaven's help was welcome in our neighborhood. We needed God's best support. It was dangerous to be on the streets. In that end of town, a gang called the Brady Street Gang had gone on a murderous rampage and had made national headlines for their tragic exploits.

One Easter, we had just returned home after the evening service. While turning on the television to catch the evening news, we caught the lead story that Sunday evening. "Thousands attended houses of worship today to celebrate the resurrection of Christ, but this man went to church for a different reason…" The cameras were rolling, and when we looked at our TV, we found they were fixed upon the annex of our church. The would-be burglar had broken into the church to steal whatever he could to feed a habit, was handcuffed and lying arrested on the floor of the hallway where precious feet had walked that very morning. I was unaware that in the next few years I would spend a good part of my life working with men like this young man. Many of those we worked with have become trophies of God's grace in the Kingdom of God. It became our responsibility to break into their lives, so cautiously guarded by a moat of suspicion, racism, fear, and dependency.

One evening, I preached an illustrated sermon on the Fruit of the Spirit. We had a fellow dress in a devil's costume, and, as I preached, he sneaked into the crowd and began to question everything I was preaching. He played the part particularly well. At given times, our fiendish foe stuck his head around a door or got up behind the big Hammond organ and vigorously shook his head in scoffing disbelief. I took large pieces of plastic fruit and spoke of each of the fruits of the Spirit, using my props as illustrations of how we are to give no place to the devil. Further in my sermon, I chased that devil through the crowd, and they simply went wild! The kids and the young people loved it. They thunderously cheered and praised God, and the sheepish devil fled from the building.

He had done this several times that night, going out a different door each time. However, the last time he went out of the building, he scurried through a side door with me hot behind him. The chase was on! This time, I trailed him right out the door into the night! Just out that door was the side street of church, and fifteen feet or so from the building, cars were always parked on the street. As he broke though the door, he screeched frantically with his jet-black, satin cape flowing like a dismal mist behind him. Believe me, he was wearing one of the most grotesque rubber masks I have ever seen. Again, he looked the part.

As we ran outside, we noticed a thief stealing the battery out of one of the cars parked just outside the door of the church. He had the cables loose and was just ready to make his getaway. Johnny, the fellow playing the devil, said when he looked up the thief was running and screaming madly down the street as fast as he could go. Heaven helped us in spite of ourselves. You could say the devil was on the run that night in more ways than one.

I have in my office what is called an Executive CRDL. This contraption has a magnet base with small pieces of metal that adhere to the top of it. Its structure is to remind one that his ideas, like the small pieces of metal, can be shaped as he sculpts them together in whatever form he chooses. Over the years, I have noticed that people (especially children) cannot keep their hands off it. And, when they have happily finished playing with it, I have found myself retrieving many of the particles of metal that have fallen to the floor or into the sofas and chairs where the novice sculptors were seated. I have been able to identify with the amusing CRDL, and have come to find them to be somewhat like pastors. Many men have attempted to shape pastors by their own expectations, and it takes a mature pastor to know how to pick up the pieces and put things right when the novice sculptors leave the room. Take heed, much of what God has invested to make pastors what they are may be lost if they set out unawares. Many hopes have been crashed down like those tiny pieces of metal from the top of the magnet base. However, I have learned to skillfully take the magnet base and sweep it over the scattered, fallen fragments. It's then that each piece of metal flies back up to the base. His Word to us must always be our foundation, our base. His truth to us will always unerringly pick up the fragments others leave behind, and it will invariably keep us convinced we are who He says we are in Him. I am reminded of the Jewish proverb, "Lord, please help me when I need to get up. I can fall down by myself."

EARTH RELATING TO HEAVEN

The great challenge of the Body of Christ is learning how to relate all that we do to all that the Father in heaven desires us to do. The challenge is compounded because the communication process between the two realms is not like anything we have on earth. There is no phone cable, internet link, or fax machine that enables us to communicate on the natural level. The problem is that we are communicating between two realms—earth and heaven. In order to speak into the heavenly realm we must learn to speak by the Spirit. God is Spirit, and heaven is in the spirit realm. That realm does not have physical dimensions like our earthly realm. Therefore, there is no need for earthly means of communication. We simply speak our prayers through our spirit and they will ascend into the heavenly realm where the Father lives. In our prayers, God is invading our realm and seeking to govern in our realm.

> The Bible begins with the heavens: "In the beginning God created the heavens and the earth" —not 'the earth and the heavens'; the heavens come first. The Bible closes with the holy city, new Jerusalem, coming down from God out of heaven (Revelation 21:2); and, just as heaven stands at the beginning and at the end, so everything in between, in the Word of God, from the beginning to the end, is from heaven and to heaven. As it is in the natural realm, so it is in the spiritual. The heavens govern the earth and the earthly, and the earthly has to answer to the heavenly. It is the heavens, it is heaven, that is ultimate: everything has to be in the light of heaven, to answer to heaven, to come out from heaven. That is the sum of the Word of God, the whole content of the Scriptures.[2]

CONVERSING WITH GOD

I have a book in my library on prayer that originally cost 79 cents. I bought it in York, England at a secondhand bookstore for less than that at today's price. The devil trembles when he sees these great books on prayer sold this cheap. In the book, the author speaks of the significance of conversing with God. One of my favorite passages of scripture is used to describe the value of individual prayer. I love this passage because it speaks of an entrance into a new understanding or view awaiting the reader.

> *Rise up, my love, my fair one, and come away. For lo, the winter is past...The flowers appear on the earth; the time of the singing of the birds is come, and the voice of the turtle [dove] is heard in our land...Arise, my love, my fair one and come away. Oh my dove, that art in the clefts of the rock in the secret places of the stairs, let me see thy countenance, let me hear thy voice; for sweet is thy voice* (Song 2:10-14 KJV).

This scripture tells us there is a place where you might rendezvous with the lover of your soul. In this meeting place, this place of transparency, God comes searching for you just as He searched for Adam and Eve in the garden.

The author had a steady grasp on intimacy with God as well. As her words poured, I realized her keen insight, and knew it must have led many into more intimacy with their loving Father. We must be reminded that it is God's will for all of us to affectionately talk with Him daily. And, God's kingdom *will come* in those private times of devotion. The author suggests several practical and very attainable points that will help you in discovering the privilege of secret prayer.

1. Have a definite meeting place to pray alone. Every time you pass that place, you will be reminded that both physical and spiritual refreshment await you there.

2. Anticipate meeting One who loves you in a personal and intimate way. Before you arrive at that place, let your mind say, "I am going to meet Him."

3. Let your prayers be semi-audible. You are speaking to a Person, and hearing your voice will keep your thoughts centered on Him.

4. Use a daily devotional book and use some kind of study book to give you needed direction in daily Bible reading.[3]

CONNECTING WITH HEAVEN

During those days in Houston, we were learning that His ways were higher than ours. He had given us an invitation to be seated with Him in high places, and we were becoming ever aware of that reality. Daily we were beginning to realize that our battle was not with the young people we longed to see set free; our battle was with principalities in high places. This was a spiritual battle, and we needed our Heavenly Father's help. Though I was taking clinical pastoral counseling classes at that time, and though I was appreciative of what I learned in regards to counseling and therapy, I understood that these acquired tools were not enough to set the captives free. It might help us understand the nature of their problems, but it would not offer the power to set them free. Oftentimes we were like the man in the story of Elijah who lost his axe head. All he was left with to bring the tree down was a wooden handle. If our ministering was dependent on counseling alone, it would be like us trying to cut down a wooden tree with a wooden handle. We would be forever pounding on that tree and never making progress, and the price would be great.

Jesus came from heaven and went back to heaven. So, we set our aspirations and desires on things above and not beneath. In doing so, our prayers took on a whole different content. We asked Him for much bigger things than we'd ever dreamed before. There is something about being in the presence of the Father that increases one's faith and makes one bold. God had invited us to ask of Him, and we discovered the reality that He actually *would* give us the heathen for our inheritance. And, excitingly, we found them right in the shadows of downtown Houston.

Jesus continually stayed connected to heaven during His earthly journey. He remained resolute even in the wilderness of temptation when the tempter tried to offer Him the kingdoms of this world. Jesus knew that ultimately they were not His to give. When the devil led Him up to the high mountain and said, "Worship me and I will give all you see to you," he was absurdly trying to bribe the Lord who created it all in the first place. Someone said the devil tried to bribe Him instead of pushing Him. If he could have pushed Him, he would have. The enemy will always have a hard time trying to defeat us if we refuse to cooperate with him. Becoming as persistent as Jesus was means we must pray as He did. Knowing this, He gave us His prayer pattern to help us in our own battles.

The writer of the Book of Hebrews puts all this in a heavenly context. Jesus has opened a way into the heavens, clearing a pathway for our communication. In fact, He sits at the right hand of the Father and puts in a good word for us. Isn't it great to have some pull in the heavenly realms! I sometimes feel heaven tugging on my heart and, when I do, I tug on heaven.

"Seeing then that we have a great high priest, that is passed into the heavens" (Heb. 4:14 KJV) we know that:

- Our High Priest can be touched by our weakness. He is very sympathetic about our cause.

- The throne is a throne of grace, not condemnation. At that throne we get the power we are seeking, not condemnation.

- As we touch the heavenly realm, a flow is created that sends mercy to us in order to deliver us from our time of trouble.

The more boldly one prays, the bolder he'll become. It's a known fact. As we prayed, heaven became as real to us as Herman Park or the Domed Stadium in Houston. Heaven is a prepared place for a prepared people. Be prepared for heavenly results when you reach out to your Heavenly Father.

One day in Houston, I heard one of the young men witnessing in a gasoline station. He asked a gentleman nearby if he was going to heaven. The fellow was embarrassed by the question, but reluctantly nodded, "Yes." Then, the man in question proceeded to tell us he went to the First Church in town (for whatever that was worth). He thought he was off the hook, but he was dealing with a bold fisherman. "Praise God!" the witness shouted without hesitation. He said, "Brother, if you are going to heaven, then you pray for me." The perplexed man turned and walked away embarrassed. Ronnie Moore, a missionary friend of mine, says, "Silence is golden. It is a yellow streak right up your back."

KNOCKING ON HEAVEN'S DOOR

Heaven's door opens quickly to those who are in trouble. Knowing where to turn in the time of trials or when you need answers is half the battle. Too often we turn to the wrong sources. In this simple prayer Jesus gave us a clue—turn your eyes towards heaven. Don't look to the wisdom of the wise or

71

the strength of the strong. When you need help, you must learn to turn your eyes upward, not inward or outward.

Stephen got a glimpse of what it is really all about. In the face of the murderous crowd that was stoning him, Stephen looked up and this is what he saw: "I see Jesus standing at the Father's right hand" (see Acts 7:55). What a comforting vision! Stephen became lost in heaven's realm. While the stones were flying at him, he had stepped over into another realm as heaven's door was opened to him.

I have heard men preach on hell. And, as angry as some seemed to be, I concluded they were full of their subject. Many of these young people were living in what they deemed to be hell already. So, the hope of a better world to come was a relevant message. This was the message I preached. I made it clear that it was not just a fairy tale. It was a hope that was real. It would not deceive them. And they desperately needed it. They ached for someone *real* to love them. They yearned for something to do and something to hope for. This hope of heaven had a way of taking their eyes off the horrible things they were often forced to endure in their present localities. After all, the end of the prayer Jesus gave us is about the triumphant end of all things. His is the kingdom. His is the power. And, His is the glory. Forever. His kingdom come, His will be done on earth, as it is in heaven. As you grow in prayer, the influence of heaven will become more real in your life.

> ***O FATHER in heaven,*** *hear thy child;*
> *The night is dark and the waters wild,*
> *And I must perish unless thou wilt heed,*
> *For cold is the night and dark, indeed.*
> *Then a small voice whispered, "Peace, be still,"*
> *And the winds and the waves obeyed His will.*

THE WINDOWS OF HEAVEN

Father in heaven, oh, hear my prayer;
My boat may sink, and I know not where;
Unless thou wilt heed my beseeching cry,
Alone I must perish, alone must die.
Then a small voice whispered, "Peace, be still,"
And the winds and the waves obeyed His will.

Father, thou hast heard and answered my call,
Thou master of the seas, thou ruler of all;
Thou never wilt forsake thy trusting child,
Though dark is the night and the waters wild.
Then a small voice whispered, "Peace, be still,"
And the winds and the waves obeyed His will.[4]

Hulda Fetzer (1906)

CHAPTER FIVE

The Kingdom Just Kept on Coming

Once Jesus inaugurated His ministry at the river Jordan, some of the first words from His lips were, "Repent, for the *kingdom* of heaven is near." Matthew announced that Jesus initiated His public ministry by traveling throughout Galilee preaching the good news of the Kingdom. This itinerant preaching throughout the tiny, backward land of Israel set up the beginning of Jesus' physical ministry on the earth. The Sermon on the Mount became His first recorded words as the new prophet on the scene. This historic word is His "State of the Union" address, and in it He sets forth the divine principles that will govern the Kingdom He has come to proclaim. It is the constitution and bylaws of the heavenly rule. With these words He set aside the existing religious order and established a new order that will be loyal and subject to the heavenly King. He brought from heaven a brand-new form of government that does not depend upon political suppression, philosophical manipulation, or religious domination. The laws of this kingdom are not contained in human words developed by rationalistic thought; they are a heavenly script written on the hearts of men.

Eternity Written on the Eyelids

I don't really know when it happened, but at some point God wrote eternity on my eyelids, and that heavenly script of the Kingdom was written across the linings of my soul. One day, a guest minister who had a campus ministry in Michigan sat in my car with me. It was my job to pick him up from the airport, and we were waiting on one of the men from our church to come and join us for lunch. Since the fellow we were waiting on was running late, we just sat and waited, making small talk and getting acquainted. The weather was humid as usual, and the temperature wasn't whispering spring, as we would have liked; rather, it was shouting summer. As the conversation went on, all of a sudden the man in the car began to weep uncontrollably. Nothing I did would console him. I felt considerably awkward in the presence of this sobbing saint.

When he finally got control of himself, no thanks to me, he falteringly mumbled, "I just don't understand. I just don't understand." "Understand what?" I asked. "*I just don't understand why they have to go to hell!*" Who was he talking about? Looking out the car window, I noticed two little children playing in the front yard of a house. Both were in white cotton underwear—a boy and a girl no more than three or four years old. And, both were incredibly filthy, so much so that the only way one could tell that what they were wearing was originally white was that their waists were still unsoiled. There was not a blade of grass in the yard. Yet, still satisfied with their meager field, they played in the dirt. My friend's heart was visibly and understandably broken over their future. He was *passionate* about the lost. And, his fervor did not go unnoticed. It touched my heart that day.

HERE COMES THE KINGDOM

You see, His Kingdom just kept on coming! It comes to us in little experiences just like the one you just read. It comes through our life experiences both in the public place with others and the private place with the Father. I have found that it also came into our lives through gift ministers God sent, many like this man, to equip us for the future. Unfortunately, we often miss our moment of opportunity of experiencing the Kingdom because we are so easily distracted by other things. Many in the Body of Christ have lost the power of observation and therefore miss very powerful truths that come to them every day.

One night, we went to the school on our bus that was called My Brother's Keeper to pick up those who would return with us to our ministry house, The Salt Inn. A loud-mouthed kid with a ball cap twisted on his head (having more hair than head) got on the bus, posing a question as he climbed aboard. He asked with slurred speech, "Hey mister, can I go with you?" I remember responding, "Sure, why not?" He then said, "I think I backslid." I didn't realize what he meant by, "Can I go with you?" He meant, literally, that he wanted *to go with us and be with us.* This young man ended up living with us for the next nine years, and he became like a son to my wife and me.

Over the next twenty years, this bright young man became uniquely equipped by God to do what I never could have done. He spoke face to face in public schools and assemblies eventually talking to more than six million young people. He related to them his story of the cruelties of his life in the ghetto. He told the youth of this nation about the sham and sorrow of their culture and, at the same time, he also showed them a way of escape, pointing the way to their path of freedom. Jacob was on a mission to change his world, one young person at a time. He was one of many through whom the Kingdom just kept on coming. I often say, *real* moves of God are generational or they are not real moves of God at all. Today, Jacob Aranza still has a national ministry and pastors a network of churches in Lafayette, Louisiana with his wife, Michelle, and their five boys.

LET US GO AND TELL THE KING'S HOUSEHOLD

Once we prayed "Thy kingdom come!" we quickly learned that what God asks you to do does not end with what God asks you to do. We were given the house for ministry, and young people started coming from everywhere. I could never understand why some church people felt threatened by what God had given us to do. Here is where we felt "The Velvet Brick." Some church people *will* stone you, but they are just religious enough to wrap the brick in velvet before they hammer you with it. We were thankful that the necessary few understood. We were overwhelmed and so excited about what God was doing in spite of the naysayer gallery sitting on the sideline. It was too much to ask to keep what the Lord was doing to ourselves.

We felt like the four leprous men in the story of Second Kings 7. Ben-hadad, king of Aram, came against Samaria and laid siege to the great city. At the same time a great famine had also hit the land. Things were so bad that they were selling ass heads and doves' dung for food. These four lepers decided that if they remained in the city they would die. So, better to go out to the enemy's camp and beg mercy. What they didn't know was that God had sent a miracle, causing the sound of chariots and horses to be heard in the Aramean camp. The enemy had all fled. When the lepers got into the camp, the enemy was gone, and they had left all of their supplies behind. As the lepers dived into the food they finally realized that they could not keep silent.

*Then they said to one another, "We are not doing right. This day is a day of good news, but we are keeping silent; if we wait until morning light, punishment will overtake us. Now therefore come, **let us go and tell the king's household**"* (2 Kings 7:9).

In similar fashion we felt compelled to tell the Body of Christ about how the Kingdom of God was coming to Houston. We were capturing the enemy's prey that had been held captive for many years. The changes in these kids' lives were astounding. This was the Kingdom at work. It was rearranging the old order and imposing the order of heaven on these communities.

OPPOSING THE FORCES OF THE DARK WORLD

Our times in Houston taught us about the power of the Kingdom and of the very real struggle that exists between the forces of light and the forces of darkness. Wherever those forces engage each other there will be a great collision. In the ministry of Jesus we see that one of the signs of the coming Kingdom is deliverance and healing. In Houston we saw the power of the Kingdom healing and delivering kids just like in the times of Jesus.

Jesus was going throughout all Galilee, teaching in their synagogues and proclaiming the gospel of the kingdom, and healing every kind of disease and every kind of sickness among the people (Matt. 4:23).

But if I cast out demons by the Spirit of God, then the kingdom of God has come upon you. (Matt. 12:28).

Don Milam describes that collision in this way:

It is totally impossible for two diametrically opposed kingdoms to exist together; one will overwhelm the other. Religion, though, has learned to coexist with the evil around it. In fact, religion has always found a way to cohabit with evil.

But it was not so with this Man or the rule that He had come to establish! He could not ignore the suffering and suppression that the enemy had imposed upon the people. Everywhere the message of the Kingdom was proclaimed, the power of that Kingdom was demonstrated. Wherever He found the smallest measure of faith, disease was rebuked, demons expelled, sin forgiven, and people freed.

That is the great contrast between the spiritual kingdom He had come to establish and the religious order that men establish. Religion can permit sin to exist and can easily ignore the oppression and pain of its constituents. Religion does not find it difficult to compromise with the forces of the dark side.

Wherever the kingdom of God is manifest, however, there is no compromise. Sin must be removed, healing must come, oppression must stop, evil must be destroyed, and compassion must reign.[1]

HEAVEN INVADES EARTH

One night while we were out with a team witnessing, we had an unusual and unplanned encounter with a young man who seemed especially challenged by our presence. He held me responsible for the intrusion into his world, which was safe only to those who were user friendly, young, Mexican-Americans (which was not a politically incorrect way of identifying their heritage at that time). As we spoke with this young man, we were not fully grasping what was taking place through us at that time. Our message was, "Repent. Change your way of thinking, we come bringing His Kingdom with us." This man understood the implications of that message. He knew that another force was impinging on the perimeter of his territory, seeking to release those who were held captive in his world. This was war.

In his book, *When Heaven Invades Earth*, Bill Johnson describes the collision that happens when light invades darkness. God's Kingdom comes and wins every time.[2]

The threatened young man could feel the intrusion of heaven into his world, and the only way he knew how to respond or counteract was to threaten back. So, he told me, "I am going to kill you." I watched as he swiftly and skillfully pulled out his knife with every intention to use it on me. I can still remember the peace resonating within me on that dark night. Little did he know, but we were as at his home there on their turf as he was. Knowing that a soft answer turns away wrath, I responded, "No, you're not going to kill me." It was disarming to him. I watched as his fences started coming down. He asked me, "Why not?" I answered, "Because I love you, and you cannot handle that." He folded up his knife and, without any sense of shame, he surrendered. That young man became an advocate for the gospel along with many others in that section of the city. This night was a turning point in both our ministry and our relationship with the drug culture that continued long after I was gone from that work. An amazed Jacob was with me that night, as well as several others who had gone with us to minister. Though he was no stranger to those we were ministering to (his mother owned Modesta's Lounge just around the corner), his faith was catapulted that night by witnessing what God could do through those who would believe and seek to advance God's Kingdom into the dark places of this world.

THE KINGDOM TAKES HOLD IN THE NEXT GENERATION

And yet, what God would do in Jacob was almost aborted. Satan almost had the victory in this young man's life. One night, he came bursting into the church just before our youth meeting. He was on fire, as we would say, and it was evident that something had happened. He was heatedly talking more than usual, and he almost hyperventilated as he tried to somehow explain himself. He sounded like a radio preacher who gasps for air between each word. This spectacle would have been totally comedic if we hadn't discerned that it was quite serious.

He told us that he had hitchhiked to church. He explained that this was because he already had over thirty driving tickets and did not want another (which a friend of mine on the police department later took care of by having them erased from his driving record). The irony was that Jacob was only fourteen and did not even have a driver's license. But, his mom would still let him drive through the East End in an old Chevy that looked somewhat like a Sherman tank. He could not even see over the steering wheel when he drove it, and he had to look through the steering wheel to see where he was pointing the long nose of the car. On that particular night, Jacob was running late and, because he couldn't get a ride, he "rode the thumb," as they say.

A guy picked him up, and Jacob decided to practice his preaching on him. The man did not like it at all. He stopped the car and said, "How do you want to die? Do you want me to stab you or shoot you?" Jacob responded, "You are not going to kill me!" The man asked him, "Just tell me why you don't think I am going to kill you." He said, " Because I love you and you cannot handle that." When he told me this I broke out in a cold sweat and the gravity of what we were doing took on a whole different meaning. That night, the Kingdom almost ceased to come through Jacob's life to the multiplied thousands of desperate youth and families God was raising him up to speak to. How do things like this transpire? I had fallen in love with my generation, and Jacob, following my example, fell in love with his.

CAN GOD TRUST YOU?

Experiences like these, of which there were many, taught us quickly from where our help came. Jesus said that He would send the Comforter, and I think we had learned what is referred to by the Greek word for Comforter, *Parakaleo*. It is a word made up of two words: *Kaleo*, meaning "to call" and *Para*, meaning "to be near." *Parakaleo* refers to calling somebody near to yourself, desiring them to help you out. Jesus was saying that I am going to send you the "Alongside One." I will no longer be able to be with you in the flesh, but I am sending One who is just like Me. How awesome is that? There is One who is with us at all times.

I can understand the demon possessed man in Mark 5:18 calling out to Jesus, wanting only the privilege of going with Him. He never wanted to go back to what he was before Jesus had set him free from the tormenting legions that had bound him. You see, God's Kingdom had come to this man and set him free from the restraints put upon him by an inferior kingdom.

In our ministry, God helped us as we cried out for help. Jesus embraced us and offered us a place at His table. We felt His empowering presence with us that made us feel bigger than we really were, and it sure scared the enemy. In ministering to the lost, we instantaneously understood our need for Jesus to be near us. All the while, we learned lessons of trust. You see, the question is not, "Can you trust God?" That is an oxymoron. Of course, you can trust God! The question is,

PRAYING THE LORD'S PRAYER

"Can God trust you?" He can trust the person who learns to pray to Him like He is their Father and not just a towering figurehead in their lives. Anna Waring wrote a poem that describes this type of trust that the Father desires in each of our lives.

When I am feeble as a child, and flesh and heart give way
Then on Thy everlasting strength with passive trust I stay,
And the rough wind becomes a song, the darkness shines as day.

We had so much to discover, but His kingdom just kept on coming. Wonderfully, God introduced to us the magnificent value of praying The Lord's Prayer, and, remarkably, this prayer will continue to expand our world. Believe me, there is power in the words! It was clear that an autobiography of prayer in the life of a believer was being written. Each of our lives is a book being written by the finger of God. Each of us, in our own unique way, is a Kingdom message to the world. My book is vast now—thick and worn. I can assure you that each page is filled with the glory of God's goodness. The paper, still, is marvelous to behold. The ink is holy golden oil.

He was teaching us—me, the kids, all who were involved in this ministry—to pray and, by doing so, we became a living part of what God had entrusted into our hands. I became preoccupied with a more earnest need for power in our ministry. We were in the thick and thin of the battle. Drugs flowed like a river into our part of town. We needed more than a little help from heaven. One afternoon while we were having a church outing, a wonderful family that was very involved in church life received a frightful phone call from the police. Their daughter had overdosed and had been found dead in her apartment bathroom. The police found drug paraphernalia beside her, and her fatal syringe filled with its deadly poison was still stuck in her arm. She had taken a fix of bad drugs and it, regrettably, took her life. The power needed to bring comfort and support to this family's situation could not just be awakened emotions and anger at what was going on in the world around us. We certainly experienced that anger, but we learned it would take much more than this. Anger at the world's condition will not change the world. The harsh reality of our lack had slapped us in our religious egos.

I earnestly prayed, "Oh God, give me power—power to make a difference." It was as if He stopped me in the middle of my petition and asked, "Why do you want power?" I spoke out loud, "I thought that was what You wanted!" Once again, I heard that still small voice, "If you keep your life clean, you will have all the power you need." Each generation prays for the same things, yet too often we fail to learn from the previous generation. Power flows best through vessels that have been cleansed by the Lord.

> But spiritual power is not the same as strong emotion and the two do not inevitably go together. 'Energy' is perhaps a better word, because beside emotional stirring there is given to the praying heart a certain drive, a dynamic impulse to go out; to do, to preach, to act. Peter and John "filled Jerusalem" with their teaching; they 'could not but speak', they felt 'constrained' and were 'pressed in spirit'. An energetic faith coupled with the moral impetus and spiritual strength to execute it's visions is kindled in the Church that really seeks her Lord in prayer.[3]

CHAPTER SIX

Thy Will Be Done

Would you have the kingdom to come indeed, and also His will to be done on earth as it is in heaven? Or would the sound of His trumpet make you run mad, afraid to see the rising of the dead, and afraid to reckon for all the deeds you have done the body? Are all the thoughts of it altogether displeasing to you? If God's will were to be done on earth, would it be to your ruin? There is never in heaven a rebel against God.[1]

W hich comes first, the chicken or the egg? There I was, hooked on using the Lord's model prayer just as much as the youth in conflict were hooked on their music and dependencies. Having no understanding of prayer patterns, I was being led into something of great significance that had a momentum all its own. Before that time, I would often offer prayers that seemed to ricochet off the ceiling, never hitting their intended target in heavenly places. It was like having a well constructed electrical cord that just went so far—far enough to inspire hope, but not far enough to connect the electrical outlet with the necessary appliance. In S.D. Gordon's classic *Quiet Talks on Prayer,* he writes:

> Electricity is a strange element. It is catalogued in the study of physics. It is supposed to be properly classed among the forces of nature. Yet, it seems to have many properties of the spirit world. Those who know most of it say they know least of what it is.
>
> Some of the laws of its being have been learned, and some of its marvelous power has been harnessed for mans' use, but in much ignorance of what it is. It seems almost to belong somewhere in between the physical and spirit realms. It furnishes many similes of graphic helpfulness in understanding more nearly much truth of the Spirit life.
>
> In the powerhouse where the electricity is being wooed into mans' harnessing, or generated, as the experts say, is found a switchboard or switch room—with a number of boards [all this is of course computerized now but the principle is the same]. Here in a large city plant a man may go and turn a switch, that is, move a little handle [or punch a computer button]. It is a very simple act, easily performed involving almost no strength. But that act has loosened the power of the switchboard out along the wires, and perhaps lighted a whole section of the city.

Gordon goes on to say that the effects are multiple, employing hundreds of operatives.

> It is a secret service, usually as far as observers are concerned. It is a very quiet, matter of fact service. But the

power influenced is unmeasured and immeasurable. Just such a switch room in the spirit realm is one's prayer room.[2]

I found that when one moves into new territory in his prayer life, he subsequently will move into new terrain in his ministry to others. It was never our intention to spoil what we were and what we had been a part of, but it sure began to pale in comparison to the excitement of what God was doing on the streets in Houston. His will was to be done in our lives, not our own. And rather than clinging to what once worked for us, we decided to step out of the box of traditional Christianity. We wanted to see what would happen if we just listened to God and obeyed Him. What a concept! If we were going to step out in this way, then we could only look to the past for a reference and not preference. The past would give us a feel for what others have done but not necessarily for what we should do. The future challenge would be to continually live in this manner. Yes, we prayed often, "Thy will be done." As we continued to pray that prayer we discovered something growing inside of us—a new dependency and intimacy with the Lord.

THE KINGDOM OF GOD IS COME WHEN THE WILL OF GOD IS DONE.

Jesus was the one who taught us to pray, "Thy kingdom come. Thy will be done, on earth as it is in heaven." On another occasion He proclaimed, "Not everyone who says to Me, 'Lord, Lord,' will enter the kingdom of heaven; but he who does the will of My Father who is in heaven."[3]

There is a very significant fact about the life of Jesus. His life was consistent with His words. What He taught the disciples in that little prayer was more than just words. They were words that had been created from the substance of His life. The prayer He prayed was the life that He lived.

It was this passion for His Father's will that drove the Lord Jesus. Listen to His words:

> *Therefore Jesus answered and was saying to them, "Truly, truly, I say to you, the Son can do nothing of Himself, unless it is something He sees the Father doing; for whatever the Father does, these things the Son also does in like manner* (John 5:19).

> *So Jesus said, "When you lift up the Son of Man, then you will know that I am He, and I do nothing on My own initiative, but I speak these things as the Father taught Me* (John 8:28).

> *I can do nothing on My own initiative. As I hear, I judge; and My judgment is just, because I do not seek My own will, but the will of Him who sent Me* (John 5:30).

He now looks at His own disciples and shares with them one of the secret keys of the Kingdom. The Kingdom will not come until men and women learn to make their lives sing in harmony with the will of the Father. Submission to the will of the Father is the single most important Kingdom precept. Choosing to yield our stubborn, self-absorbed human will to a higher will—the will we rejected in the Garden of Eden—is the doorway through which the Kingdom comes and dwells among men.

The world witnesses, even if it does not understand, that another "government" is present when it sees ordinary men and women voluntarily choosing to lay aside their own plans and choices to walk in joyful obedience to their God. God's people have been called to model the reality of heaven in the earth realms by the way that they allow their lives to be merged into the will of God.

GROWING IN THE PRESSURE

I soon came to the realization that many people did not necessarily appreciate a message that makes a demand upon them, that calls out for change. Change is hard and scary. We like our secure and safe places that have been carved out over time. We don't like it when anyone starts rocking the boat. In fact, a lot of good men have been killed by that boat-rocking business.

Nevertheless, my heart burned to share what God was teaching me, but who had ears to hear? I wanted to tell the world that the Father was in the process of reviving the church. He longed to save it from being smothered to death by dogmatic and dormant lifestyles. I just knew that God wanted to turn the Church in another direction. He was standing at the gateway to their hearts, longing to partake in a living and loving connection with them. Although all of this was very true, and so very wonderful, I became aware that there would always be distractors—those who will stand in the way of what God wants to do. Not everyone will share your joy when you discover a spiritual reality that has changed your life. There will always be the cynics and the critics.

You see, there are a great number of people who would love to see God's work stagnated and who devilishly dedicate their lives to what we call *trying to abort the plans of God*. The more I grew, I found that doing His will was becoming clearer to me, and, with all this going on around us, it was wise for us to press more and more into God. As we pressed in, we found rest. It is in that secret place where your faith becomes ignited for the task that God has given to you. Taped in the front of my Bible for many years was a poem that describes what we went through for those several months. It describes, for me, what the Lord was using in those days to create a greater dependency on Him as my Lord and Savior. Those pressures were melting my will and causing it to flow into His will. The two wills were becoming one will—the will of the Father.

"Pressure"
Pressed out of measure and pressed to all length
Pressed so intently it seems beyond strength
Pressed in the body and pressed in the soul...
Pressed in the mind till the dark surges roll.
Pressure by foe and pressure by friends
Pressure on pressure till life nearly ends.
Pressed into knowing no helper but God,
Pressed into loving the staff and the rod.
Pressed into Liberty where nothing clings
Pressed into faith for impossible things.

Author Unknown

I was pressed into a daily prayer life. E. V. Hill was once heard to say, "There are two kinds of people that you deal with in ministry. Those that you pray for, and those that keep you praying." Real pastors understand what he meant by this profound statement. The question should be: "Which one of these two kinds of people am I?" Pressure became a way of life. I love how *The Great Book* describes Paul's agony in chapter 1 of his second letter to the Corinthian church. He speaks of both pressure and condemnation.

The burden was heavier than we could carry, he felt like he would die. But something happened to make us put our hope upon God (who raises people from death) and not in ourselves (2 Cor. 1:8b-9).[4]

A key principle I held onto early in life is this: I will not just try to do all the good I can, but I will also do as little harm as I possibly can. It was God who put this principle in my heart, and it was God who led us into a more excellent understanding of His will for our lives and our future.

My pastor continued as our "kneeling example" of how a man of God should pray. From his example, we learned that God really is the rewarder of them who diligently seek Him. You see, we started praying, "Thy kingdom come in the East End," and we saw it. Now, the constant prayer on our lips was, "Thy will be done." It became astoundingly evident to us that His kingdom must come before His will is done, and we were seeing that His kingdom was coming through our willingness to allow His will to be manifest in our lives. Andrew Murray spelled it out this way:

> Because the will of God is the glory of heaven, the doing of it is the blessedness of heaven. As the will is done, the kingdom of heaven comes into the heart. And wherever faith has accepted the Father's love, obedience accepts the Father's will.[5]

MAKING GOD'S WILL, MY WILL

God had been teaching me for several years about the Father/son relationship He affectionately purposed for us. One lesson occurred when we served in an earlier pastorate. A church in another town called us to be their pastor, and I thought it would be a wonderful opportunity for us to pastor a church just outside one of the larger cities in America. Looking back, probably the only reason they wanted us was because my wife could sing and play the piano, the two together being more than an asset for their body. The invitation was on the table, but we were extremely restless as we struggled to

PRAYING THE LORD'S PRAYER

make a decision. They called and told us of their congregational decision on a Sunday morning. Yet, I was ever aware of the thick cloud of grief that had been in our house the previous evening. It was as though God had "short-sheeted me." Not willing to pay the price of disobedience, I told them we were honored they asked us to come, but we could not accept their offer. *His will* always involves *His peace.* Beware of the places where there is no peace.

People often ask me how they can determine the will of God for their lives. It is our part to pray our will out of the way, and His to bring His will into action. We must knuckle down and be willing to go to that place of surrender with God, no matter what it takes to get us there. A friend of mine says it like this, "God, if You treat all Your friends like You treat me, I am surprised You have any friends at all."

Well, sometimes the things we experience have nothing to do with God. If we choose to go off on another path then we will encounter some ugly things. On the other hand, it is true that when you follow God and make His will to be your will then there will be some pain and rejection and sorrow. It is the price we must pay as we seek to impose His government on a world that has rejected Him. The inimitable C.S. Lewis described the voice of God in our circumstances in this way: "God whispers to us in our pleasures, speaks in our conscience, but shouts in our pains: it is His megaphone to rouse a deaf world."[6] The voice of God that speaks of His will is often best discovered in our pain.

There are a few things I will always do to determine if the choices I am making are in the will of God. First, I ask:

- What is the last thing God has asked me to do, and is He giving me new direction?

- Am I following the path that leads to peace in my heart, with my family and the Body of Christ in mind?

Then, I consider various factors:

- Once I have made a major decision, I do everything I can to disturb the decision that has been made. If it goes undisturbed, I then move forward, knowing God is with me.
- Knowing that my wife has a nesting nature is another thing that becomes a factor. When she is in agreement with my decisions, our unity in a matter becomes a force in itself.
- Finally, I have a few choice friends and confidants who have soaked my life in prayer, and their counsel has always been appreciated and considered.

Before I fully understood the reality of an actual will of God for my life, my intentions were simply to climb the proverbial "ladder of success" in the organizational system of church denomination. This is something I never had a class in, and I really don't think is intentionally taught. However, it *is* something one learns by observation. This opportunity to pastor a larger church in a larger territory would have definitely been a bigger rung, and I easily could have leaped over two or three on the way up. Thinking the will of God was only a geographical place, and having no idea it was a meaningful relationship, I became vulnerable to heeding other's voices, rather than the Great Shepherd's. Despite all my errors in my rationalizations, however, God had something else up His sleeve. The church asked me why I wouldn't come to be their pastor, hoping we would reconsider. Ten years later, I met someone from that church and found out they were still curious as to why I had not accepted their invitation.

You see, on the morning in question, GayNell and I had absolutely no peace on going to this place. Yes, everything they had to offer was far more than we had ever received in ministry—salary and provision. However, I told them what I felt God spoke to my heart, "As a congregation, you voted yes. But, God voted no! And, He is still in the majority when it comes to His church." The day was awful. I felt guilty for even looking at another opportunity. You see, I deeply loved my church and the people I served. But, when this incident arose, I simply felt like an unfaithful husband. I knew I had to get out of the trap of performance and ladder climbing I'd been in. I also knew the courageous act I needed to do next. I would discover in that step that the will of God would never take you where the grace of God cannot keep you.

A STEP INTO THE UNKNOWN

Following God will sometimes mean that you will have to take a step into the unknown. Following God is not for the faint of heart or the calculating soul. In my passion to do the will of God, I was about to take one of those steps.

In those days, everybody came to church every time the doors opened unless, of course, they had fallen off a horse on their head or had been hit by a car. I had something to say to my congregation in regards to the work my Father was doing in my heart. So, that night I spoke up. Everyone was there for the evening service, and I told the congregation all that had transpired. I read them my letter of resignation as their pastor as well. They were in a state of undeniable shock, and so was I. This was not my plan. However, it was His. *His* will be done.

"What are you going to do?" they asked. There were questions in regards to my future coming from all around me. One lady, having two brothers in the ministry and knowing the ropes, met me at the door on her way out of the church that evening. I have never forgotten what she said, "I sure hope you do better yourself." That was exactly what I intended to do. You see, I had peace in my decision to leave, but no peace concerning my lack of planning. As I closed the door on this stage of my life, I had no idea if there would ever be another door.

The following morning, I was up at the crack of dawn attempting to figure out my next step. While taking a bath, I had an unwelcome visitor—you know, that little "second-guessing devil" who will come and sit on your shoulder, accusing and confusing you all the while if he can. His vile thoughts started parading through my mind. "You have blown it this time! What are you going to do now that you have stepped off the ladder? You have *not* stayed with your plan." Come to think of it, I'm sure hell was throwing in its best just to sabotage and wreak havoc on my decision. Pitifully, I heard myself agreeing with that shameless liar out loud. "You're right, I *have* blown it."

A sense of despair and woeful dread started permeating the room. All at once, I felt like pheasant under glass. It was as if I had been shoved into an inescapable vacuum, where the air was still and devoid of expression. I heard not even the faintest sound, and all thoughts and suggestions were drowned out with a wonderfully authoritative stillness. God spoke to me and said, "You are my son. What can be better than that?" The security given by God of just being His son was a revelation no man has ever been able to shake. For the first time in years I was not preoccupied with the work I was to do or not to do for God. No, I did not know what the future held. However, I now knew in an even grander way who held the future—my future. As the Lord directed us into this new way of life, and as He guided us away from what we considered to be security, we found ourselves having a peace not based upon external circumstances. We found out what it means to enjoy His kingdom within—righteousness, peace, and joy in the Holy Spirit.

It was within the next year that the mighty work with Houston's youth began to develop. How many times have we planned our steps, only to have the Lord lead us in different directions of *His* choice and purpose? There I was, in a Holy Ghost schoolhouse where many lessons were to be learned. He was preparing me for His service, and, along with His Kingdom, His instruction just kept on coming as well. You see, during those years it was my conviction that each service had to outdo the last service. And, I found several things happening to me as a result of this kind of thinking. The most destructive was the temptation to minister as a result of pressure to succeed instead of ministering out of His presence.

When living this way, one finds he begins to think he is loved on the basis of performance rather than on the foundation of God's grace. For me to be what God desired to make me, I would have to learn that failure is never fatal or final as I walk in His grace. I had ignorantly given guilt a free ride for years by always condemning myself by constantly comparing myself to others, if nothing else. This mindset caused me to be guilt-driven, which causes a believer to live subjectively instead of objectively. When you live subjectively, you incessantly place yourself under the probing microscope of what other people think. This is how the lethal disease of "man-serving" gets a hold of good men and women. And yet, if we discerningly live objectively, we then place ourselves in God's hands, fully knowing we are the apple of His eye, and it is His *good pleasure* to give us the Kingdom. Again, without His grace sustaining us, we are doomed to a shallow life of pleasing men rather than God.

Having so much to learn, our classroom in knowing the will of God was 24/7. And GayNell, being the daughter of a preacher, thought it best she be my teacher. Granted, we had a few disputes along the way. And, granted, 99 percent of the time she was right. However, the greatest lesson I would learn from her over the years is that I would have no more of a ministry to His Bride than what I have to my own bride.

CHAPTER SEVEN

On Earth as It Is in Heaven: The Father Heart of God

He had a dream, and behold, a ladder was set on the earth with its top reaching to heaven; and behold, the angels of God were ascending and descending on it (Gen. 28:12).

And He said to him, "Truly, truly, I say to you, you will see the heavens opened and the angels of God ascending and descending on the Son of Man (John 1:51).

There is a certain intrigue and interest that exists between heaven and earth. While men are trying to get to heaven, heaven is trying to get to man. Jesus walked out of the gates of heaven and descended into the earth-regions of man so that he might be able to lift him up into the heavenly places. Jacob's dream illustrates the powerful connection that exists between the two realms. There was divine destiny upon

Jacob's life, and heaven was seeking to help him fulfill that destiny.

Heaven is more than just fascinated with life here on the earth. It is the will of the Father that heaven's order be duplicated in the earth. In the Garden that order was rejected, and throughout the history of man we have seen the tragic results of that decision. The great saint John Chrysostom wrote that Jesus did not say, "Thy will be done in me." It was the Father's desire that His will be done *in all the earth* in the same manner that it is done in the heavens.

> And again, He hath enjoined each one of us, who pray, to take upon himself the care of the whole world. For He did not at all say, "Thy will be done" in me, or in us, but everywhere on the earth; so that error may be destroyed, and truth implanted, and all wickedness cast out, and virtue return, and no difference in this respect be henceforth between heaven and earth. "For if this come to pass," saith He, "there will be no difference between things below and above, separated as they are in nature; the earth exhibiting to us another set of angels."[1]

HEAVEN COMES TO EARTH THROUGH THE FUNNEL OF FAITHFULNESS

Contrary to popular belief, every minister has *two* ministries. He has his *ideal* ministry, which can be vastly different from the reality of what he actually has; then he has his *actual* ministry. As long as a pastor is obsessed with his concept of the ideal, and as long as he neglects what is in front of him and chooses to remain caught up with what *could be*, then the opportunities for ministry that he has in the present will suffer. However, when he spends his time ministering in the *now* of God, faithfully watering the field that God has given him, his *ideal* ministry will then become a *reality*. You must work with what you have to make it become what you want. We must be faithful with the little, so that God will give us rule over much. I had a friend named Ebbe Bolin in Osha, Sweden who taught me this.

In 1951, Ebbe graduated from Moody Bible Institute in Chicago. Trained and ready to conquer the world, he moved back to Sweden to start Biblien Institutet (Bible Institute). The first year he had three students. He told me about them. One was sharp and called of God, the second was not bright but not dim, and the third was mentally challenged. Aware of his insignificant beginnings, Ebbe notified God that he had decided to give up. He told God he could not believe he had gone through all the work, preparation and—oh yes—sacrifice, for just these three inconsequential students. "I expected more help from You than this!" When God finally responded, He shook Ebbe's world. "Ebbe, if you don't take care of these three I have given you, I will never give you any more."

Heaven Comes to Earth Through Blessing the Generations

Thirty years later, Ebbe is still teaching and influencing the lives of young people who will impact their world for God. And yes, he took good care of the three. God entrusted him with hundreds more over the years. Ebbe's life is a marvelous example of the rich history of someone who prayed, "Thy will be done on earth as it is in heaven." As a matter of fact, it was a prayer experience that brought Ebbe and me together.

I was ministering at the school in the beautiful mountains of Mora, Sweden, situated high above a beautiful lake. The school is located in the Dalchalia Province, where the national symbol of Sweden, the Dalchalia horse, gets its roots. My staying there would be one of those unforgettable encounters that changed me forever. The snow was already postcard-picture deep and still falling. Some locals could be seen passing on horse drawn sleds, and moose would nonchalantly commute through the campus parking lots at will. For a Southern boy, it was as though I had been placed in a surreal situation.

The school had prepared lodging for me in Ebbe's office, and my bed was actually in his personal library. While getting situated, I picked up a book entitled *A Man of Like Passions*. Once I began to read it, however, I could not put it down, weeping as I read it through the night. I have never been able to find that book again, but the extraordinary message of the book was branded on my heart. As I read, I was stirred as I began to understand how Elijah devotedly poured his life into Elisha. It dawned on me just how remarkable Elijah's heart was as he became a spiritual father figure in Elisha's life. Elijah is the only prophet in the Old Testament who raised up a spiritual son of Elisha's caliber. These two prophets stand as a powerful testimony of how heaven comes to earth through fathers who are committed to investing in the next generation. Heaven will never come to earth without that kind of devotion. Elijah's influence was generational, and Elisha lived with a double portion of what mighty Elijah knew in his life. Unlocking the wealth of the next generation will bring heaven down.

I found myself ascending into the high places of spiritual reality as I considered these possibilities. There I was in that quaint library in Mora with the snow and wind whistling outside, literally devouring the truth of what God meant to be one of the cornerstones of my ministry. He, in no uncertain terms, showed me how He intended for me to follow Elijah's example and to pour my life into others as Elijah did. This would be my calling and mandate from my Father. As I continued to respond to the will of the Father, He would keep His kingdom coming into my life. I had already been training young men, but I did not realize how consequential my taking them in really was. Everything I had learned up until that point was by trial and error.

When I left Sweden I had a definitive job description that has never left me until this day. God used coaches to lead me in that general direction, and I longed to serve others as I had been served.

Fathers Who Carry the Kingdom in Their Hearts

When I was six years old, there was a wonderful director and coach of a local boy's club who took an interest in my brother and me. Even then, the thought was in my mind that, "When I grow up, I want to be like Ira DeSazo and Rudy Garcia." They made us feel like we were the most important kids in the world. We were known as the latchkey kids because our parents were not home when we got out of school. We spent our afternoons at the Panther Boy's Club in Ft. Worth, Texas. They made a definite difference in my life.

There were other coaches who inspired me along the way as well. But in my freshman year of high school, a coach walked into our lives who would have a major impact on my life. I learned to *leave it all on the field* as a result of his example. His name was Elo Nohavitza, and he had played football at Texas A&M. Coach, as I still call him, was an outstanding player who received conference and national awards for the way he played the game. His character was that of excellence, and once again God used someone (even though Coach didn't realize it) to put it into my heart and mind that when I grew up, I wanted to do something like he was doing. Who were these men, and why did they have such an astounding influence on my life? I'll tell you. They were father figures. And today, I am highly grateful for the time they invested in me. Today, Coach wonderfully lives and breathes personal evangelism. He has a consuming passion to win men and women for God, and his compassion pours from him like warm rain on dry ground. He still plays the game of life using the principles he taught so many young people. "Don't ever walk off the field with a loser's limp," he'd say. "And, leave it all on the field."

God has many different lessons He wants to teach us. By the way, He does not grade on the curve. He put great men and women in my life, and their spiritual experiences and revelation had a great impact on my life. The spiritual truths that I am walking in today are a result of their spiritual input into my life.

It is clear that the apostle Paul understood the place of fathers in the Body of Christ. "For if you were to have countless tutors in Christ, yet you would not have many fathers, for in Christ Jesus I became your father through the gospel." (1 Cor. 4:15). It is easy to impart information to students and go home at the end of the day. But true fathers are more than teachers, and their schedule consists not only of school hours. They are on call at all hours and they are more concerned about their sons growing up into maturity than they are about them just getting some information. If I was to produce in ministry sons who would follow on to know the Lord in an even greater aspect than I, I would have to take care of what God was entrusting me with as well. Once the reality of being *His son* really dawned on me, my greatest joy from then on has been that God is *my* Father. Because I was His son, I could cry out "Abba Father!" Offer anything else to me and it would still pale in comparison with having that type of understanding of the love of God. I wanted all to know this love of the Father. It is the foundation of all ministry.

ABBA! ABBA! ABBA!

In the winter of 1980, I spoke at the National Media Conference held at Smyrna Church in Gothenburg, Sweden with my friend Erland Stromqvist. While there, God reminded me of what He alone had been teaching me for nearly a decade. Hundreds of people had gathered into the old, historic church founded by the legendary Levi Pethrus. The congregation was pregnant with a rich passion for God and a fervent desire to reach the lost. When I concluded the time of personal ministry, a Scandinavian man with a shrill, tenor voice began to cry out high above the roar of the hundreds who were crying out for God to use them. He bellowed, "ABBA! ABBA! ABBA!" Turning to my friend and interpreter Erland, I asked, "What is he saying?" He said, "Don't you know?" We stood in the midst of hundreds of men and women as we were conversing in muffled whispers. "No, I don't or I would not have had to ask you. I thought it might be Swedish." He said, "No, it is Aramaic. He is crying out FATHER! FATHER! FATHER!"

That man will never know how God used him that night to speak to my heart and to punctuate with his personal appeal to God the cry of my own heart. Sometimes we need to be reminded of what He is teaching us on our journey. To know our Father personally and in an intimate way will always be the most important lesson for us to learn. Knowing and experiencing the Father on a daily basis is the key to heaven coming to earth. We must always be aware that He is our sufficiency. If needed, he will remind us from time to time.

Life seems to come in seasons. Life is like the ocean with its ebbs and flows. Sometimes, I feel like that Arabic child Robert Summers saw fall in the streets of the old city of Jerusalem. It happened one day when he was visiting the tourist market. On the moment of impact, the wounded child began to cry, "Abba!" The child continued running down the street, crying out "Abba!" with every step. Summers is a tall, lanky Texan. With steady determination, he decided to follow the child to see how this melodrama would play out. The injured child took three strides to Robert's one as he ran through the crowded, narrow street. Little did the child know he had an audience of one, and little did he know that he would change a life forever.

There were others on the streets, but because of their interest in *things* rather than *experiences*, they missed a great lesson. Summers' perception and curiosity was satisfied when the wounded child finally fled into the doorway of one of the little shops. My friend watched as a large, mustached Palestinian shop owner quickly leaped out from behind a crowded counter toward the child. The boy's father bent over and took his son up into his strong arms, held him to his chest, and comforted him with the loving assurance that the boy would be okay.

The crying ceased and so Robert walked away enriched by this real-life human video of a son's sincere need of a father's genuine love. Some sons in the Kingdom know that the Father's house is always a safe bet when they come to the end of their rope. However, that is not the only thing God longed to teach me. God showed me that to live in the Father's blessing is wisdom, and that only coming to Him when I was in trouble was folly. He will always be there for me in my time of trouble, but He wants to be there for much more than providing an escape hatch for every time I get into trouble. There was so much He wanted to teach me and show me. I had to ascend to a higher level than just living with a prodigal's mentality. If God were to share His great life with me, I was to give Him an outlet—my heart and my mind and my life.

You see, if I had not learned more of the Father's heart, I may have been content, though I was not a prodigal, to live like the elder brother. He lived in close proximity to the house, but never really enjoyed the full benefits of what could have been relished. He took it all for granted. He was a son, but he lived like a hireling.

God saved me again this time. He saved me from the mindset of just being satisfied with working for the Father, but never being able to celebrate His abundant life. His love is without bounds toward all, and abundant life in God is more than a possibility to those who would believe. Our Father's intention is that our relationship with Him be a continual feast—a king's feast.

So, pray that His Kingdom will come. Pray that His will be done. If you do, the Father will take you at your word, and you just might see heaven come down and the Father's heart revealed through you.

CHAPTER 8

Thy Name, Thy Kingdom, Thy Will

Our Father, which art in heaven
*Hallowed be **Thy name***
***Thy kingdom** come*
***Thy will** be done*
On earth as it is in heaven

Hallowed be *Thy name!* Andrew Murray says,

> There is something here that strikes us at once. While
> we ordinarily first bring our own needs to God in prayer,
> and then think of what belongs to God and His interests,
> the Master reverses the order. First, *Thy* name, *Thy* king-
> dom, *Thy* will; then give *us*, forgive *us*, lead *us*, deliver
> *us*. The lesson is of more importance than we think. In
> true worship the Father must be first, must be all. The
> sooner I learn to forget myself in the desire that He may
> be glorified, the richer will be the blessing be that prayer

will bring to myself. No one ever loses what he sacrifices for the Father.[1]

Have you ever noticed how most men strive to make a name for themselves? They are willing to suffer much in the ministry. No matter, as long as *their* name is lifted up. However, when I entered into a partnership with God in the streets, I quickly realized people could care less what my name was. My task was to make *His name* known in the East End. Furthermore, it was already hard for most people to say my name. And, it was not any easier for those with thick barrio accents to pronounce it. So, I became Brother Keith. Those young men wanted to experience the forgiveness and reality of a living, loving, and all-powerful God. Their problems were real, and they desperately needed Jesus. We, in turn, brought Him to the streets of downtown Houston.

HOLY FIRE

Because of the significance of this work, we learned very early on to do what we called *praying the Word*. And due to our heart for God's work on the streets, we became preoccupied with praying for revival. We were more concerned for what God wanted to do to honor His name on the streets than what we wanted to do to make ourselves known. We pleaded with God, asking for the fire of revival to come like a blazing inferno that consumes a forest. Have you ever tried praying like this?

Oh, that You would rend the heavens and come down,
That the mountains might quake at Your presence—
As fire kindles the brushwood, as fire causes water to boil—
To make Your name known to Your adversaries,
That the nations may tremble at Your presence!
When You did awesome things which we did not expect,

You came down, the mountains quaked at Your presence
(Isa. 64:1-3).

We prayed for God to come down, and come down He did. He triumphantly ignited our hearts like fire burns brushwood. Have you ever seen brushwood blaze? The blaze of fire takes place rapidly and leaps from one place to the next, causing a ghastly incineration wherever it goes. These fervent flames are almost impossible to keep under control. You've seen it. Brushwood is like kindling you use to ignite a fire. And, with all God was pouring out, we knew it to be only the beginning. This would spread. This would advance. His Kingdom would come. Oh, how we loved being His kindling for the blaze of revival that He wanted to bring. Only, let Him stay close. We must never let His fire in us turn to ashen cinders.

We prayed as did the prophet Isaiah, "Come down as fire when it causes water to boil" (see Isa. 64:2). Accordingly, the fire fell. We felt the heat in more ways than one. And, I hold fast to the belief that God loves to turn up the heat, since a lukewarm vessel has never really done that much for Him. His fire fell, coming down in ways that were irresistible. His name was made known by the miracles that happened. The fire of heaven consumed us and our clothes smelled of fresh fire from the heavens. Our countenance changed, retailored to that which would be more pleasing to Him. All around us knew we had been with our Master. And, as He revealed His name, His Kingdom, and His will to us, we continued to fan the flames. "More, Lord" was our heart. "We want still more of You."

It is one thing to see God move in a controlled environment like a church meeting. But it is altogether something different when you see Him move in an unobstructed, non-church setting. It is sad to say that controlled settings are about all that most people have ever known. And yet, we saw firsthand the wonders of God working outside the church. We were taking the prophetic fire of God to the streets. We were empowered with boldness—a flame, and a shamelessness in us that wet blankets have never been able to snuff out. The name of God was being honored on the streets as people saw a living demonstration of the power of God for the first time.

MAKE HIS NAME HOLY

The Greek word for "hallow" is *hagiazo* and means "to make holy" or "to sanctify." Jesus tells us to pray, "Let Your name be sanctified." *Sanctify* can mean "make holy" or "treat as holy." Now we know that we can't make God holy, for He is holy. Therefore, it means to *treat* God as holy. God's name has great importance to Him. His name is wonderful, and we should never take it lightly. The psalmist lends us help in understanding the importance of the value of the name of the Lord.

And those who know Your name will put their trust in You, for You, O Lord, have not forsaken those who seek You (Ps. 9:10).

Ascribe to the Lord the glory due to His name; worship the Lord in holy array (Ps. 29:2).

O magnify the Lord with me, and let us exalt His name together (Ps. 34:3).

Sing the glory of His name; make His praise glorious (Ps. 66:2).

His name shall endure forever (Ps. 72:17a KJV).

Give unto the Lord the glory due unto His name: bring an offering, and come into His courts (Ps. 96:8 KJV).

Moses and Aaron among His priests, and Samuel among them that call upon His name; they called upon the Lord, and He answered them (Ps. 99:6 KJV).

He sent redemption unto His people: He hath commanded His covenant for ever: holy and reverend is His name. The fear of the Lord is the beginning of wisdom: a good under-standing have all they that do His commandments: His praise endureth for ever (Ps. 111:9-10 KJV).

I will worship toward Thy holy temple, and praise Thy name for Thy lovingkindness and for Thy truth: for Thou hast magnified Thy word above all Thy name. In the day when I cried thou answeredst me, and strengthenedst me with strength in my soul (Ps. 138:2-3 KJV).

Because of our faith in God and our obedience to Him we created honor for His name. Where His name was blasphemed on the streets we sought to bring honor to that name. We prayed *in* His name and *that* His name would be known in the East End of Houston. We did what we had to do in His name, and God helped us. After having seen the mighty, incalculable works of God in that setting, I understood John's heart when he said all the works Jesus did were too numerous to write about.

THY NAME, THY KINGDOM, THY WILL

The Qaddish is one of the oldest and most used prayers in Jewish piety and is the prayer that is prayed in the synagogue at the end of every service. The numerous echoes in late biblical, apocryphal, and early rabbinical sources attest its popularity in pre-Christian Palestine. The similarities between the passion and the words of The Lord's Prayer and the Qaddish are quite amazing. It is as follows:

Glorified and sanctified be God's great name through-out the world which He has created according to His will. May He establish His kingdom in your lifetime and during your days, and within the life of the entire House of Israel, speedily and soon; and say, Amen.

May His great name be blessed forever and to all eternity.

Blessed and praised, glorified and exalted, extolled and honored, adored and lauded be the name of the Holy One, blessed be He, beyond all the blessings and hymns, praises and consolations that are ever spoken in the world; and say, Amen.

May there be abundant peace from heaven, and life, for us and for all Israel; and say, Amen.

He who creates peace in His celestial heights, may He create peace for us and for all Israel; and say, Amen.

One can sense the earthly appeal of God's people in both prayers as they long for the coming of the Kingdom, the vindication of His name, and the accomplishment of His will. The prayer of the Qaddish and the prayer of Jesus are words that have been etched into the hearts of God's people down through the ages. Joachim Jeremias says,

> These petitions are a cry out of the depths of distress. Out of a world which is enslaved under the rule of evil and in which Christ and Antichrist are locked in conflict, Jesus' disciples, seemingly a prey of evil and death and Satan, lift their eyes to the Father and cry out for the revelation of God's glory. But at the same time these petitions are an expression of absolute certainty. He who prays thus, takes seriously God's promise, in spite of all

the demonic powers, and puts himself completely in God's hands, with imperturbable trust: "Thou wilt complete Thy glorious work, abba, Father.[2]

HIS NAME EMBODIES HIS WORD

Praying The Lord's Prayer took on new meaning to me day after day. I began to understand even more the worth of praying as Jesus taught His closest associates. I found that His name was embodied in His Word, just as the Old Testament names of the Father personified the revelation of what God was like. As Jesus taught His disciples to pray, I discovered that His supplications were tied to Old Testament revelations of the Father's name. We saw His followers praying in His name like the Old Testament believers prayed for the exaltation of the Father's name. In downtown Houston, we tied this all together and prayed God would help us keep His name holy as well. Our hearts were like that of a family member who would protect, by his illustrated integrity, his family's name.

A question arose in my heart while I meditated on this interaction between Jesus and His disciples. Why would one of His disciples ask Him to teach them how to pray anyway? He prefaced his inquiry with the fact that John the Baptist taught his disciples how to pray. Can you imagine what John taught them? We know they fasted and prayed. But, we have no record of what he taught them. Still, John would have done well to keep his faith high in regards to what the Holy Spirit showed him. Bear in mind that he, old and imprisoned, sent his disciples out to Jesus with a faithless question. He asked, "Are You the Messiah, or should we look for another?"

Jesus patiently told them to go tell John what they had seen, and His answer to John was all encompassing. Though John's inquiry was unbelieving, Jesus' response was full of power! He purposefully intended that John know the truth of who He was, once and for all. "The blind see, the deaf hear, and the lame walk. Those with skin diseases are healed, and the dead are raised back to life again. The poor have the gospel preached to them as well." Jesus spoke life to that imprisoned evangelist. The forerunner of the Messiah had fresh fire poured upon him. He now knew, beyond a shadow of a doubt, that Jesus was *the* confirmation of all he'd preached.

REVELATION IS ISOLATION'S CONSOLATION

Yes, John the Baptist, the cousin of Jesus, had once heralded with *great conviction* the coming of the Lamb of God. He declared that this Messianic King would bring the Kingdom of God with Him wherever He went. Can you see it? The truisms John preached in the wilderness were being gloriously fulfilled by the one he baptized in the Jordan! How marvelous. And now, Jesus was the one who must increase while John decreased. Jesus' message to John gave his life meaning. Jesus was the answer to John's ministry in the wilderness. You might only think of John as leather lunged and isolated in a wilderness setting. However, he quickly learned a great mystery: Revelation is isolation's consolation.

Jesus is the personification of perfection. And yet, He understands our humanity in every way. The reason we have amazing results using His prayer model when we pray is that He became our High Priest. Have you ever considered before this what gave Him the license to teach us to pray? In Hebrews 1 we read,

> *God appointed His Son to speak to us [...] the Son is the shining brightness of God's glory and the exact picture of God's real being. The Son holds up the universe with the power of His word. He has provided a cleansing from sin, He has sat down at God's right side in heaven* (Heb. 1:1-3).[3]

116

The writer of Hebrews goes on to share what God proclaimed about His Son:

Your throne [...] lasts forever and forever, You rule your kingdom fairly. You have loved what is right and hated what is wrong. This is why God, your God, has made you king over your friends with the oil of gladness (Heb. 1:8-9).[4]

The reason we were effective in praying as He taught us was that we knew He was our mediator, sitting at the Father's right hand. He was not a distant God, and He continually revealed to us the person of who He was in our lives. When we realized the magnitude of praying for the rule and will of the King in our life, His fire fell. His name was glorified. His will was done. Alan Redpath, in his book *Victorious Praying*, says:

Furthermore, He has a perfect knowledge of the human heart. 'He needed not that any should testify of man: for He knew what was in man,' said John. He himself is perfect man. His knowledge of our sorrows, of our temptations, of our problems, and of our needs is absolutely perfect. For in visiting this dark world of ours, in entering our human life and in dying our death, He suffered as we suffer. 'We have not an high priest which cannot be touched with the feeling of our own weaknesses; but was in all points tempted like as we are, yet without sin.'[5]

We became increasingly restless as we prayed with this burning revelation and in this momentous manner. *His* prayer branded my heart, and I could not pray without it being the filter for all other prayers. It was as if I were being moved into His purpose for my life *through* praying this prayer. This restlessness took hold of me daily, and I did not know it was God stirring my feathered nest. I had found what I considered to be my niche in the ministry, but He was not going to allow me to become too comfortable. Looking back, I have discovered that if I had remained in my comfort zone, I would have stolen the destiny from those who would follow in what God used us to initiate. There was a process I found myself in, and countless others have found themselves in this process as well. I was satisfied with a divine dissatisfaction. An old poem voices well what would have become a way of life for me, had I not responded favorably to God's direction in my life.

"The Tame Ole Duck"
To me my soul is a tame ole duck
Dabbling round in barnyard muck
Fat and lazy with useless wings
But sometimes
When the North wind sings
And wild ones hurdle [sic] overhead
It remembers something lost and dead
Cocks a wary bewildered eye
And makes a feeble attempt to fly
It is fairly content for the shape that it is in
But it is not the duck that it might have been.

Author Unknown

Chapter Nine

Daily Prayer for Daily Bread

At the end of World War II, many grievous children became orphans in desperate need of care because they lost their parents in the blitzkrieg bombings of Great Britain. In one orphanage where several of these children had been plucked from the street, it was difficult to deal with them because of the uncertainty in their minds. They would cry themselves to sleep. Concurrently, they'd often be found sobbing and weeping through the night. The caregivers did not know what to do to comfort these children who were clearly in such great distress. One evening, however, they gave each child a piece of bread. Upon receiving the bread, the children's constant weeping ceased, and they quickly fell asleep.

God has never wanted any of His children to live with uncertainty in their life. As a good Father He is prepared to meet our needs. It is true that we cannot effectively pray "Our Father" with the mindset of an irresolute orphan, timidly facing a formidable future. Children are never bashful about making requests of their parents and neither should we be bashful.

It is also true that if you are moving forward and coura-geously following your passion in God, there will always be a sense of the unknown before you. There will be times when you walk through dark, wilderness places. It is sad that there are those who have foolishly chosen not to leave the security of their surroundings in order to avoid the possible hardship of launching out into the unknown places. Living in God's Kingdom requires that His citizens are willing to walk by faith. His Kingdom becomes a reality in our lives when we choose to walk by faith and not by sight. It is not natural for the soulish man to pray for God's Kingdom to come. The longing for the manifestation of His Kingdom is not a prayer born out of the heart of man, but out of the heart of God. God is the one who etches the words on the plates of our heart and eventually transforms those inscribed words into verbal words that are prayed with great desire.

The Lord's model prayer is one of forward motion, and He shows us that what we lack is to be asked for on a daily basis. It is ours to understand what His bread actually is. And, He implores us to take, eat. We would all do well to partake. Hence, it is best you grasp the following words in context, or your conclusion will only become a pretext.

> One time Jesus was somewhere praying. When he stopped, one of his followers said to him, "John taught his followers how to pray. Lord, please teach us how to pray, too." Jesus said to them, "When you pray, pray like this: 'Father, may Your name always be kept holy. May Your kingdom come. Give us the food we need each day. Forgive us of the sins we have commit-ted; because we, too, forgive everyone who has done wrong to us. And keep us away from temptation'" (Luke 11:1-4).[1]

(I have noted that this was the account of Luke and not of Matthew. It is important to do this because Luke, not being

120

an eyewitness on the scene, only records under the inspiration of the Holy Spirit as he sees the events through the disciples' eyes.)

> *Then Jesus said to them, "Suppose one of you went to your friend's house in the middle of the night and said to him, 'A friend of mine has come into town to visit me, but I have nothing for him to eat. Please give me three loaves of bread.' [Note: Verse 6 was combined with verse 5 above.] Your friend inside the house answers, 'Go away! Don't bother me! The door is already locked. My children and I are in bed. I cannot get up and give it to you.' I tell you, perhaps friendship is not enough to make him get up to give you the bread. However, he will surely get up to give you what you need, because you are not ashamed to continue asking"* (Luke 11:5-8).[2]

PERSISTENT PRAYER GETS THE BREAD

Jesus' emphasis on *persistent, nagging* prayer was a concept that was very familiar to those who lived in the culture of that day. People often traveled at night to escape the suffocating heat of the sun, which reached boiling temperatures in some places. So, it was customary for these travelers to knock on certain doors, in the middle of the night, if they had need of bread. What made this intrusion difficult in most cases was that the slumbering family lay together on bedding spread out on the floor in one room. Imagine the commotion it would make if you lived like that and someone knocked on *your* door begging for bread. Let's just imagine the encroacher was a friend. Your answer would still be the same, "Don't bother me, we are down for the night. The door is padlocked, the security system is on, and I don't want to wake up the house. If I open the door to you, I will never get these screaming kids back to sleep."

Friendship has its boundaries. Many would absolutely not get up solely because a friend was knocking at the door. A person probably would, however, get up if the banging was incessant, and if the person would frankly just not go away. So, in His prayer, what do you think Jesus was teaching them? It's simple. To follow Him, you will have to live a life of endless, constant prayer. When reflecting on Jesus' given petition, I realized I have always prayed this prayer with several wonderful biblical truths pushing through to demand my attention. I am reminded, "Man does not live by bread alone" (Deut. 8:3,) and that "[Man lives] on every word that proceeds out of the mouth of God" (Matt. 4:4).

We all know that God is not mute. He speaks to us by His Son, who is the Bread of Life. And, throughout my walk I have found the offering up of this prayer has continually changed me. Praying in this manner brought me to a place of absolute dependence upon God. The bread that I longed to eat was His will—I longed to know and do the will of my Father. I am so grateful that I am not alone. The multifaceted revelation of the power of praying in this manner with a pure heart has changed the course of other lives as well. The following excerpt applies to this pertinent and highly effective prayer, and is adapted from *Streams in the Desert*, volume II.

- I cannot say "Our," unless I am aware that I am not alone in the presence of God, but united with God the Son and God the Holy Spirit.
- I cannot say "Our" if I am shut up to the circle of my own concerns and interests, and refuse to listen to the voices of my brothers and sisters in the family of God worldwide.
- I cannot say "Father" apart from the Savior-hood of Jesus Christ and acceptance in Him as God's Son,

and apart from the inner witness of the Holy Spirit of adoption.

- I cannot say "which art in heaven" without realizing that I live on earth, where the focus of rebellion to the will of God is headed up.

- I cannot say "Hallowed be Thy name" unless I am prepared to take action in specific situations that dishonor the name of God in my life, my home, or in my nation.

- I cannot say "Thy kingdom come" unless I am ready to fight the enemies of God's Kingdom and go to lands where God's Kingdom still needs to come.

- I cannot say "Thy will be done" if there are any reservations in my heart concerning God's will for my life.

- I cannot say "On earth as it is in heaven" if I am not prepared to sacrifice anything in my heart and life that is tainted by the spirit of the world.[3]

I would add to the list above:

- I cannot pray "Give me this day my daily bread" if I am content to remain where I am spiritually and am not prepared to move on in God to the things He has prepared for me—things eyes and ears have not seen.

- I cannot pray "Forgive me my trespasses" if I am not prepared to forgive others their trespasses against me, remembering every act of forgiveness and mercy is an act of God.

- I cannot pray "Deliver me from temptation" if I willingly and continually grieve the Holy Spirit by not obeying the Word of God.

PRAYING THE LORD'S PRAYER

PRAYING FOR OTHERS AS YOU PRAY FOR YOURSELF

As God redirected me leading me further into His purposes for my life, the most selfish thing I could do would be to pray for my own needs to be met and fail to pray for the needs of others.

Looking back, I remember a remarkable woman who attended our church during those years in the East End. When she spoke, her words shot like a bullet into the atmosphere with a highpitched shrill. Her last name was Tweedy, and we called her Sister Tweedy. She was only about five feet in stature, but she was a giant in God. Sister Tweedy lived unselfishly, and she lived to share the gospel through tract distribution everywhere she went. I remember her at bus stops passing out the good news. I can but imagine, but only God knows the reward He had waiting for her. She is long gone on to her reward today or I would not be allowed to tell this story.

One night, before we moved away from Houston to the heart of Texas, we were having a revival service. All of a sudden, I felt compelled to go directly to the Salt Inn, which was located not far from the church. I was on the platform and preliminaries were finished. I just got up and left without telling anyone where I was going. When I pulled up in front of the house, a desperate young man was on the porch. It was quite clear that he was about to break in through the front window. He actually had his fist drawn back, excitedly ready to crash through the glass. He interrupted his movement only when he heard the sound of my voice, which most of the time sounds more like a throaty growl.

With the glass still in one piece, this distraught young man informed me he had come for help. I took him back to the church with me only to find out he had a hidden rage that was about to manifest. As soon as we got inside the office at the church, he exploded. Since no one knew where I was or why I had left the building, it was just he and I. Finally, someone came looking for me. When they found me, I told them to immediately go and find Sister Tweedy. When they brought her to my office, I pulled her aside so no one could hear us, asking her secretly, "Sister Tweedy, have you been fasting? I need the help of someone who has been fasting." She humbly acknowledged she had been, and I asked her to help us pray for the tormented young man. He was a tall, lanky fellow who had family connections with one of the most notorious motorcycle gangs in the South, so I was completely shocked by her request. She boldly asked us to leave the room, resolutely assuring us she would be okay if left alone with him.

We slowly walked out of the room. But, within five minutes, she opened the door and magnificently exclaimed, "Cleddie, you can come in now!" We walked in and found the young man now more sober than a bridegroom on his wedding day. Due to the powerful anointing on Sister Tweedy's life and the tremendous relationship she had with the Lord through prayer, this once demonized fellow had been marvelously set free.

A few weeks later, I baptized him in the bathtub at the Salt Inn. The next thing we heard, he had tragically burned to death in a trailer fire. What if no one had left the platform that night? What if Sister Tweedy had not been fasting? What if Sister Jamison had not heard the Lord speak to her to give us the property with one stipulation, *that we work with young people?* What if we had not prayed that week, "Thy kingdom come in the East End of Houston?" What if GayNell had not said, "Someone needs to do something with these young people" that night on Allen's Landing? I will never cease to be amazed at the mysterious ways that God leads His people.

Though we had stepped out into a pathway that appeared to be camouflaged and uncertain, the road led us to learn even more about praying The Lord's Prayer. J.Oswald Sanders says:

> Dependence on God's supply, "Give us this day our daily bread." Although we have our own needs, we are to be concerned about our needy brothers, and should ask nothing for ourselves that we do not ask for others.
>
> Bread is referred to as the stuff of life, a staple necessity. In this context it may stand for whatever is necessary for daily life—our temporal needs. "Daily" can here also mean, "for the coming day." If we offer the prayer in the morning, it covers the day already begun. If in the evening, it covers the following day. The meaning is clear. We are to ask God's provision for the immediate future. We are to live one day at a time, in dependence on His gracious supply. In doing the will of the Father, Jesus found satisfying food to eat of which His disciples knew nothing (see John 4:32,34).[4]

OUR BREAD FOR TOMORROW, GIVE US TODAY

The two "we-petitions," for daily bread and for forgiveness, hang together as closely as the two "Thou-petitions" honoring the name and crying out for the Kingdom to come. They are like bookends to The Lord's Prayer. One focuses vertically upwards towards heaven and the other glances horizontally towards the needs of man.

The Catholic theologian Joachim Jeremias, in his research on The Lord's Prayer, says that the commentary on Matthew written by Jerome in the fourth century concludes that the literal rendering of this verse is: "Our bread for tomorrow give us today."[5] For centuries the word translated "daily" made scholars a little confused as to its meaning. This is the only place that word occurred inside or outside the

Bible. A few years ago, an archeologist dug up a papyrus fragment that contained a housewife's shopping list. Next to several items the woman had scribbled this word for daily. It probably meant, "enough for the coming day." The phrase should be translated, "Give us today bread enough for tomorrow." When prayed in the morning, it is a prayer for the needs in the hours ahead. Prayed in the evening, it is a request for the needs of the next day. The implication is, of course, that God will supply what we need to honor Him and do His will.

We turn our eyes away from our own hands and look to the Father in heaven requesting that He supply us with all that we will need tomorrow. We do not know what will happen tomorrow, but the Father does. In a spirit of trust we ask the Father to give us what He alone knows that we will need for tomorrow.

I AM THE BREAD OF LIFE

I am the living bread that came down from heaven. If anyone eats of this bread, he will live forever. This bread is My flesh, which I will give for the life of the world (John 6:51 NIV).

While they were eating, Jesus took bread, gave thanks and broke it, and gave it to His disciples, saying, "Take and eat; this is My body" (Matt. 26:26 NIV).

There is another way to look at this prayer, and the two interpretations are not adverse to each other. Jesus declares that He is the Bread of Life and that anyone who eats this bread will live forever. Is it possible that Jesus was also teaching His disciples the necessity of praying to receive that portion of Christ that they would need every day? He is our sustenance, our life. At the last meal that Jesus had with His disciples, you will remember that He gave them bread to eat, saying that it was His body.

THE GOD OF ALL ABUNDANCE

Christ never meant that we were to live the Kingdom life in the energy supplied by our own strength. He expected that His disciples would learn how to eat of that heavenly bread that would give them the strength for the journey. He invited them to come to the table often and partake of His life.

The prayer of dependence on God far outweighs the prayer for just enough to get by. I am reminded of a native group on a certain island who worshipped the moon. When missionaries came to them with the gospel, they asked them why they had chosen to worship the moon. The people of the island replied, "It is because the moon lights up the night. What would we do without moonlight in the dark of night?" Take heed, fear has a way of choosing gods for us. What these islanders did not know, however, was that the moon would have no light to give without the sun. I believe God loves to provide for us, but we must also bear in mind that His supply is not limited to insipid daily rations. His pantries are quite huge, and He delights to give to us from His abundance. "And God is able to make all grace abound to you, so that in all things at all times, having all that you need, you will abound in every good work" (2 Cor. 9:8 NIV).

WHAT GOD PROVIDES IN MERCY, HE WILL PROVIDE IN POWER

Jesus' timeless story of the prodigal son helps us realize there is more to His Kingdom than what many perceive. In this story, we see the possibility of living in the Father's house without ever having enjoyed the full benefits available. Even though a person truly has a relationship with the Father, they can still miss out on God's best. Look at the elder brother. He was a son who manifested great displeasure toward his Father when his prodigal brother returned, wonderfully welcomed home. The elder brother exemplifies the type of person who never realizes that failure is never fatal in grace. If you have a limited opinion about what God will provide for you *in mercy*, you will have a limited opinion of what God can provide for you *in power*. In Psalm 78, we are given some idea of the table God provided for the children of Israel in the wilderness. They are pictured for us with food in their mouths. And yet, in the midst of their provision, they forget and turn back, limiting the God of Israel.

"May those who delight in my vindication shout for joy and gladness; may they always say, 'The Lord be exalted, who delights in the well-being of His servant'" (Ps. 35:27 NIV).

Take the limits off God! Those islanders had to come to the place where they shed their old concepts, realizing that the moon has no light without the sun. In like manner, we have a poverty mentality that must be shed—a mentality that believes that God can only give us *just so much* and never *more than enough*. There is a lot more on the Father's table than just the crumbs that fall to the floor. It is a crumbly faith that is content to be on its hands and knees picking up the little crumbs on the floor rather than sitting at its rightful place at the table. He is the Bread of Life! Healing is the children's bread! He is the Bread of Presence! And, His body is the Bread of Remembrance. He is the one who took and blessed the bread from a little boy's lunch bucket—enough to feed 5,000. He is the Bread of Heaven that can feed your hungry soul. As the light of the Father's great love for us begins to dawn, we will begin to see that God really wants to provide for us in life and ministry. He is not limited in what He can do *in* us, nor is He limited in what He can do *through* us if we only believe.

FINDING BREAD FOR TOMORROW

What a thrill, however, to be changed hour by hour, day by day, week by week, and month by month. The way one prays can change his life so that he can fly into the high places of God and enjoy the abundant gifts of the Father. There are some things you will discover on your own. However, God has also made it clear that we are to faithfully share with others the lessons we have learned and the spiritual realities we have seen. I want to pass on these truths that were learned so many years ago on the streets of Houston. I don't want you to come to the end of your life regretting what might have been.

The work in Houston had thrived for several years when God began dealing with me about change. He shared with me that He now wanted me to go to another assignment. I could not believe it. The need was so great here, and the ministry was doing so well. Others had taken on greater responsibility, and I was giving more time to other ministry demands. I loved what God had given us to do; I loved the people around us and loved the excitement of ministry. I remember a night when a young man named Ray came through the back door of the church with just a suitcase in his hands. Many we came to know lived that way, entering our lives with everything they owned jammed into one broken old suitcase. With us then pointing them to the capable hands of Jesus, what was not to love? People who really needed help reached out to us night and day. Here is the problem. Without knowing it, subtly our identity was being wrapped around what we were doing, and to leave this work was a horrifying thought. But we knew we had heard God. The Father would give us our bread for tomorrow and he would supply the needs of those we left behind.

LOVING THE WORK OF THE LORD OR THE LORD OF THE WORK

The night I was leaving town, I felt like a deserter. Who would fill the place of ministry? Who would step in to what God had started? The only thing I knew was that God was leading us away from our beloved Houston. But for what reason I had not the slightest idea. I sent my family on ahead that afternoon with the moving van, and I followed that evening, pulling a U-Haul trailer that carried the remainder of our belongings. I wept over the city as I left. I wept over the ministry God had given us. As the miles rolled by, I asked God to make my eyes a fountain for tears like those of Jeremiah, and He obliged me. I was glad I was by myself, or I would have been so embarrassed. Then, in the middle of my musings, I heard the Lord ask me a question. It was simple and to the point. "Did you love *Me* as much as *what I gave you to do?*"

For the next two hundred miles, I did not speak a word. I didn't say a thing. I pulled over and spent the night with His probing question resonating in my mind. All these years later, that question has lived in my heart. It is so easy to love the work of the Lord more than the Lord of the work. And we must all be sober and vigilant in the work of God's Kingdom, lest we fall into that trap. I carried that question in my heart for several years before I attempted to answer it.

What about you? Do you love what you are doing more than you love Him? Answering this question will help you live with far less stress in your life than you could ever imagine. It was a simple thing to love those who had nothing but love to give us back. It was effortless to love those who made no demand on us but to love them. It was so easy to share our life with those who had so little. But would we love God more than these? I learned firsthand what the psalmist meant when he said, "To the hungry, every bitter thing is sweet." In the end all we could pray was, "Thy will be done." And whether

He required us to make still another move or not, we were in it for the long haul. We desired His Kingdom more than our own. We prayed that the Kingdom would come, and when it came, we obeyed.

CHAPTER TEN

The Most Frequently
Prayed Prayer

God is a forgiver. And if you are going to be a qualified co-worker you will have to be a forgiver as well. God never puts a finger on our past, except to heal it. If we are truly forgivers, we cannot put our finger on the past of others who have wronged us. It is God who lavishly gave us His only unique Son, whose ultimate act on the Cross was the supreme manifestation of forgiveness. The absolute proof that Christ is Lord of your life is revealed in your willingness to choose to live in forgiveness. Remember, whatever a person sows or plants, he will reap. If I sow tomatoes, I will reap tomatoes. If I sow corn, my harvest will be corn. If you sow forgiveness, you will get forgiveness, but if you sow judgment and criticism and un-forgiveness, that is what you will get in return.

According to the law of sowing and reaping to reap forgiveness, I must sow forgiveness into others. An old preacher's saying is profoundly simple and simply profound. "Hurt people hurt people, forgiven people forgive people, and loved people love people." Isn't it remarkable as we see Jesus teaching His disciples to pray what He would ultimately demonstrate on the cross at His crucifixion. When you pray "Forgive us our sins as we forgive those who sin against us," remember the cross.

Andrew Murray said that as bread is the first need of the body, so forgiveness is the first need of the soul. *Forgiven*—this is our position as we look towards heaven. *Forgiving*—this must be our posture as we look towards the earth. You cannot offer to others what you have not first received from the Father. Until you have drunk from the pure streams of God's forgiveness, you cannot give a drink of water to others. Unfortunately, too many of God's people are trying to offer what they have never experienced, and the gift is therefore tainted with our own sense of rejection.

FORGIVEN AND FORGIVING

Jesus struck at the very core of the trouble in the human heart when he sounded these words. Much of the heartache in today's world is a result of an unwillingness to forgive ourselves and to forgive others. Have you considered the unprecedented value of praying this prayer on a daily basis? First of all, it cannot be prayed in a familiar and rote manner, oblivious to what we are praying. It can be frightening and difficult to pray this prayer! You may have even silently asked, "Will my prayers be answered if I pray using The Lord's Prayer as a model for my personal prayer life?" The Lord will hear your prayer if it is prayed out of a passion that is birthed in an understanding of the rich reality of the words you are praying. If it is just words you are speaking, thinking that there is magic in the words, then the prayer will have no power. Speaking the prayer should revive within us memories of our moments of unforgiveness. In his book *The Lord's Prayer*, Joachim Jeremias says:

> With these words he who prays reminds himself of his own need to forgive. Jesus again and again declared this very point that you cannot ask God for forgiveness if you are not prepared to forgive. God can forgive only if we are ready to forgive. "Whenever you stand praying, forgive, if you have anything against any one; so that your Father also who is in heaven may forgive you your trespasses"(Mark 11:25). At Matthew 5:23-24 Jesus even goes so far as to say that the disciple is to interrupt his presentation of the offering with which he is entreating God's forgiveness, if it occurs to him that his brother holds something against him; he is to be reconciled with his brother before he completes the offering of his sacrifice. In these verses Jesus means to say that the request for God's forgiveness is false and cannot be heard by God if the disciple has not on his part previously cleared up his relationship with the brother. This willingness to forgive is, so to speak, the hand which Jesus' disciples reach out toward God's forgiveness.[1]

PRAYER AND THE LAW OF FIRST MENTION

One of the principles of biblical interpretation is the *law of first mention*. This means that when you are seeking to understand a certain biblical truth you should always go back and examine when it was first mentioned. Often in that passage you will discover great clues regarding understanding that particular truth. When we come to the issue of prayer, we know that there are twelve words for prayer in the Old Testament and seven words used for prayer in the New Testament. The first time prayer is mentioned in the Bible is Genesis 12:13, where Abram prays that Sara will tell the Egyptians she is his sister. The word used for prayer here in the Hebrew language is *Na*. This is also associated with *Ana*, which means "I pray thee." The Greeks used this word when they exclaimed *Hosanna*, which means, "O, save us." In a careful review of the use of this word, we discover that it was always used in desperate situations.

Abram said to Sara as they approached the border of Egypt, "I pray thee (or, *Na*)." He said something like this, "Do you know how beautiful you are?" That set the stage for the next request. "The Egyptians are going to kill me so that they might have you if they know you are my wife. So, just tell them you are my sister." Abraham is a little desperate and thus his prayer. We must always remember that man's extremities are God's opportunities.

Think of Jacob crying out for blessing after pulling an all-nighter wrestling with the angel. Think of what it *cost* him. Accordingly, think of what it *brought* him. Once Jacob, he became mighty Israel. Though drained and exhausted, and although he limped away toward the rising sun, he was undeniably a man who saw the face of God. Like someone said, "Don't trust anyone without a limp." Jacob assiduously clung to the angel for a blessing. He no longer wanted to live in deceit, and so his was the fervent prayer. In each of these places, the man of God was in a predicament, and as he called out for his divine rescue, God heard him. He will also hear you as you speak from your heart asking your Father to forgive you. In the power of that forgiveness you are now enabled to go forth and forgive.

JOSEPH AND THE AMAZING TECHNICOLOR DREAMCOAT

One of the greatest stories in literature is the story of Joseph and his brothers. My wife and I were privileged to see the stage production of Andrew Lloyd Webber's *Joseph and the*

Amazing Technicolor Dreamcoat in the theater district of London. The production was stunning, and it was an evening we will never forget. Nevertheless, there never would have been a production had there not been a Joseph. Over the years, I have given a lot of thought to the saga of his life. His is a marvelous story of forgiveness played out in the human arena. His story could be very familiar to many stories today. Great damage has been done in many families because of jealousy, anger, and abuse. While poring over the story time and again, I've come to realize some things which help me when I pray: "Forgive me of my trespasses as I forgive those who trespass against me."

It all starts in Genesis chapter 45. In this passage, we find that after what seemed like a lifetime of adversity and disappointment, Joseph is now standing before his brothers, who started his downward journey into Egypt. Years had gone by, and I am sure that the brothers had often thought about their pernicious actions against Joseph. A decade and a half of Joseph's slavery was always on their minds. Still, God had a plan. At this point of Joseph's story, these are the spiritual truths I discovered about forgiveness:

- Then Joseph could no longer control himself before all his attendants, and he cried out, 'Have everyone leave my presence!' So there was no one with Joseph when he made himself known to his brothers" (Gen. 45:1 NIV).
  There is PRIVATIZATION when it comes to forgiveness.

- Joseph wept out loud and everybody in the house heard it. "I am Joseph! Is my father still living?" (Gen. 45:3 NIV). When true forgiveness is given, there will always be a lot of catching up to do.

There is VULNERABILITY when it comes to forgiveness.

- Joseph's brothers were speechless and dismayed at his presence (see Gen. 45:3). True forgiveness has a way of taking you by surprise.

  The necessary ingredient of true forgiveness is ASTONISHMENT, not ARROGANCE.

- Joseph was not vindictive or controlling. "And now, do not be distressed and do not be angry with yourselves for selling me here" (Gen. 45:5a NIV). He knew as long as they were angry with themselves they had not forgiven themselves.

  He used NON-INTIMIDATION. Joseph had learned this in the previous years when he was overlooked and forgotten.

- Joseph knew life was not just a "you and me thing" going on. He brought Sovereignty into the picture. "You meant this for evil but God meant it for good" (see Gen. 50:20).

  This is PROVIDENTIAL LEADERSHIP. So, to cooperate with His providential plan for my life, I must learn to live with the "forgiveness switch" on all the time.

- Joseph's brothers had not grown spiritually as he had through all the things he experienced. Always remember, jealousy will prohibit spiritual advancement. God will continually put you in situations where you can learn to be your own person. "And Joseph said unto them, Fear not: for am I in the place of God?" (Gen. 50:19 KJV). Joseph knew if he would not forgive his brothers, it would be the same as thinking he was God over their lives. And, he knew better than that. People may have been impressed with Joseph, but Joseph was not caught up with being impressed with himself. Rather, Joseph comforted his brothers and spoke to their hearts. **He had the REALIZATION that forgiveness will affect others, not just the parties where there has been an offense.** You see, Joseph was to save not only his brothers, but he was "to save many people alive." How many people have been held back from God's Kingdom coming into their lives because they harbored some stinging unforgiveness in their heart?

Joseph's brothers, though awestruck, knew they longed to face the music of another day. Interested in saving their own skins, they sent word to Joseph. That word was *Na!* "Please forgive the trespass of your brothers!" They knew he was a man of principles. Joseph would not bring greater sorrow to his father's heart by harming them while Jacob was yet alive. But his brothers were still not sure what Joseph might do to even the score after their father was gone. Shocked by their own gruesome dealings, they agonized over the torment Joseph must have experienced in that deep pit in which they had slung him years ago. Their thoughts were strained and torturous. Feeling the debt they owed, they asked him indirectly for his forgiveness. God had already done a deep work in Joseph. The answer to that request had been forming in Joseph's spirit for many years. Now was the time for him to respond as his brothers fearfully stood before him. Reaching out to embrace them, Joseph forgave all.

A DRAMATIC STORY OF FORGIVENESS AND HOPE

One of the most incredible stories of forgiveness I have ever heard is the story of Pat Vandenburgh. Pat had always been an outstanding athlete. He simply loved sports. However, when his mom died of cancer he lost interest in sports and desperately tried to fill that vacuum in his life by medicating the loss with alcohol. Though he had always been a leader, even his friends recognized that he was different. He found himself at a loss although one girl had once told her mom that "When Pat comes around, it just seems we all have a sense of peace." That peace was no longer there. One night, that same girl was riding along with another friend in a car Pat was driving. He was not able to navigate a turn in the road and, as a result, the young lady was tragically killed. Pat was placed in a Department of Corrections facility in northern California.

While miserably serving his time, Pat had a dynamic conversion. He then used the remainder of his sentence to memorize most of the New Testament. One day while he was incarcerated, he read a newspaper from his hometown. His eyes fell on a story about a church trying to evangelize the high school he once attended. He wrote the pastor of this church a letter, commending him for his effort. He also shared with the pastor that he had attended that very high school, and that no one had ever witnessed to him about Christ in the years he was there. The pastor was so moved by the letter that he chose to read it the next Sunday morning, which just happened to be Easter. What the pastor did not know was that the family of the girl who was killed that night while Pat was driving drunk attended his church and were in the service that morning.

At the close of the service, they approached the pastor and asked him for the letter. For several months they corresponded with Pat. During this time, however, Pat was unaware that they were the parents of his deceased friend. Finally, they told him who they were and arranged for a meeting. Pat, of course, was fearful as the time for the meeting approached. You see, this had been their only child and, sadly, Pat knew this to be true. The day for the meeting finally came. During that meeting the family told Pat of what was happening in their life and that they forgave him for what had happened to their daughter. Today, they will tell you how much they love Pat and his family. This is an extremely special story about some very special people. The power of forgiveness has a way of producing people like that. The family, drawing on the love and compassion of God, mercifully offered a pardon to Pat. Later when his parole hearing took place, the family was there to represent him and beg forgiveness of the judge. Pat was released and is one of the finest husbands, fathers, friends, and ministers of the gospel I know. Forgiveness puts an end to all of our struggles to reconcile our past. It opens prison doors to freedom for both the offended and the offender.

FORGIVENESS OPENS DOORS TO NEW DIMENSIONS OF MINISTRY

Have *you* ever had a hard time forgiving anyone? I have a dear friend who was done a great injustice by someone in denominational authority over his life. One day he called me, telling me more than a few times that he just could not forgive this man. I felt impressed to tell him to write a letter, forgiving the man, and then just let it go. That is exactly what he did. It turned out that the man in question was eventually exposed for a moral failure in his life. My friend did not gloat over the failure of the man, for he knew and had great admiration for his family. Contrarily, he grieved over the man. And the moment my friend chose to release the man from his resentment, God opened new doors that led him into the most fruitful ministry of his life.

When the *head* is sick, the *whole body* is sick. This friend of mine, though very discerning and prophetic in nature, was so loyal and loving that a multitude of sins had been undetected by those he ministered to. Today, however, he is now able to minister to people of all cultures in a trans-denominational setting. Looking back, he knows God providentially led him into his present ministry. Looking back, he knows God's way is the way of forgiveness.

When you pray according to His pattern prayer, things will begin to take place on earth as it is in heaven. Notice how the big issues in our lives are embodied in this simple outline of prayer given us by the Lord himself:

1. Our Father—PARENTAL LOVE
2. Hallowed be Thy name—GOD'S PRESENCE
3. Thy kingdom come—LIFE'S PRIORITIES
4. Give us this day our daily bread—PROVISION
5. Forgive us—PARDON
6. Lead us not into temptation—POWER FROM ON HIGH
7. For Thine is the kingdom, power and glory—PRAISE[2]

Personally, The Lord's Prayer has been like pieces of a puzzle coming together over the years. I was staying in a home recently, and the lady of the house had chosen to decorate the walls with pieces of art that were actually puzzles which had patiently been put together. These puzzles were then placed in appropriate frames, becoming a unique complement to a lovely home. Some people's spiritual lives are like a puzzle with pieces still missing. However, as you learn to pray this prayer, the pieces begin to come together, and your life becomes a beautiful portrait of the power of forgiveness. May the Master continue till that portrait is completed in each one of us.

CHAPTER ELEVEN

Prayer for Power

I AM NOT ASHAMED OF THE GOSPEL OF POWER

> "And lead us not into temptation,
> but deliver us from evil."

Is it possible that God would lead us into temptation? How can that be? If not, then what does the verse really mean? We cannot effectively pray the prayer until we understand what we are praying. Albert Barnes in his notes on the New Testament will help blow away the smog of uncertainty in this verse:

> And lead us not into temptation. A petition similar to this is offered by David, Psalms 141.4: "Incline not my heart to any evil thing, to practice wicked works with the workers of iniquity." God tempts no man. See James 1:13. This phrase, then, must be used in the sense of "permitting." Do not "suffer" us, or "permit" us, to be

143

tempted to sin. In this it is implied that God has such control over the tempter as to save us from his power if we call upon him. The word "temptation," however (see the note at Matthew 4:1), means sometimes "trial, affliction," anything that "tests" our virtue. If this be the meaning here, as it may be, then the import of the prayer is, "Do not afflict or try us." It is not wrong to pray that we may be saved from suffering if it be the will of God. See Luke 22:42. Deliver us from evil. The original in this place has the article—deliver us from the evil—that is, as has been supposed, the evil one, or satan. He is elsewhere called, by way of eminence, the "evil one," (Matthew 13:19; 1 John 2:13,14; 3:12.) The meaning here is, "deliver us from his power, his snares, his arts, his temptations." He is supposed to be the great parent of evil, and to be delivered from him is to be safe. Or it may mean, "deliver us from the various evils and trials which beset us, the heavy and oppressive calamities into which we are continually liable to fall."[1]

An ancient Jewish evening prayer that was prayed during the time of Jesus sheds further light on the meaning.

Lead my foot not into the power of sin,
And bring me not into the power of iniquity,
And not into the power of temptation,
And not into the power of anything shameful.[2]

WATCH AND PRAY SO THAT YOU DO NOT ENTER INTO TEMPTATION

It is clear that Jesus' prayer does not mean that leading us into temptation is an *action* of God, but it is His *permission* that allows things to happen. It is a prayer asking God that we be preserved from succumbing to temptation.

In the garden, Jesus said to His disciples, "Watch and pray, that ye *enter not into* temptation: the spirit indeed is willing, but the flesh is weak" (Matt. 26:41 KJV). A great storm was brewing on the horizon, and the disciples were totally unaware of the danger swirling all around them. With these words of caution to the disciples Jesus rings the bell, sounding the alarm. "Pray, pray, pray." As we face the storms of life, prayer should be our immediate and automatic response. Walking down life's pathway we can pray, "Oh, Father, do not let me be drawn into the torturous web of temptation's pull."

How does one pray when faced with temptation and trials? Well, what we need to do is take a little walk with Jesus in that garden. Follow Him to the place that He carves out in the garden and listen to how He prays. "And he went a little farther, and fell on his face, and prayed, saying, O My Father, if it be possible, let this cup pass from Me: nevertheless not as I will, but as Thou wilt" (Matt. 26:39 KJV). Now we have the key for our verse here in The Lord's Prayer. From the prayer of Jesus we find the key to understanding this portion in the Lord's Prayer. This is how we pray: "Lord, do not allow us to enter into temptation and trials. If it is at all possible deliver us from the hour of trouble and the web of the evil one. But, if there is no other way, then we cry out to You to empower us for that hour and deliver us from the evil around us and give us grace to walk through the evil around us."

In the end, this final petition is not asking God to preserve us from temptation but to preserve us in the temptation. In writing to the church at Corinth, Paul hits the nail on the head when he encourages the saints with these words:

> There hath no temptation taken you but such as is common to man: but God is faithful, who will not suffer you to be tempted above that ye are able; but will with the temptation

also make a way to escape, that ye may be able to bear it (1 Cor. 10:13 KJV).

In the midst of trials we are not left alone. God is with us and, in the midst of the trial, He will supply an abundant supply of grace so that we may escape it. It is important to notice that the escape is not rapture from the trial but support in the trial.

The Lord's Prayer is found in Matthew 6, and when taking the entirety of the chapter in context, we see Jesus is dealing with various aspects of prayer and fasting. A couple of these thoughts will add to our understanding of this prayer.

"WHEN YOU PRAY..."

Prayer was another thing the Lord expected of His followers, which may account for Him abruptly questioning His disciples that fateful night when He asked, "What, could you not watch with Me one hour?" Again, Jesus often taught from the Old Testament scriptures concerning present revelation He gave to the twelve. One day, His disciples observed him overturn the tables of the moneychangers and the chairs of them who sold doves. Jesus fearlessly exclaimed, "My house *called by My name* shall be called a house of prayer of all nations. But, you have made it a den of thieves!" Looking back into the Book of Jeremiah, we find a similar situation. The prophet, speaking for God, voiced a searching question,

> *Will you [...] come and stand before Me in this house, which is called by My name and say (by the discharge of this religious formality) we are set free, only to go on in your sin? Has this house, which is called by My name, become a den of robbers in your eyes (a place of retreat between acts of violence)?* (Jer. 7:10-11 AMP)

The eternal results of Jesus driving the moneychangers out of the temple are absolutely astounding! Notice that "the blind and the lame came to Him in the temple, and He healed them" (Matt. 21:14). When He made a stand for the Father, His kingdom came. I will now leave you to draw the conclusion of what happens when we make God's house a *house of prayer.*

"WHEN YOU FAST..."

Jesus did not make it a question of *if* but *when* when it comes to fasting. The assumption drawn is that all believers are expected to fast. My mother fasted every Thursday for thirty years. Thursday was her day of fasting. Growing up, I was never aware of her life of fasting. However, one day she and I were talking and she shared with me the value of fasting in her personal life. Take note: I do not think fasting is a way to gain leverage with God any more than I think you can bribe God with a gift. But, He calls us to fast. Hence, I will say fasting is of the Lord.

I have found that Isaiah chapter 58 gives us incredible insight into the kind of fasting that pleases the Father:

> *Is not this the fast that I have chosen? to loose the bAnds of wickedness, to undo the heavy burdens, and to let the oppressed go free, and that ye break every yoke? Is it not to deal thy bread to the hungry, and that thou bring the poor that are cast out to thy house? when thou seest the naked, that thou cover him; and that thou hide not thyself from thine own flesh? Then shall thy light break forth as the morning, and thy healing shall spring forth speedily; and thy righteousness shall go before thee; the glory of the Lord shall by thy reward* (Isa. 58:6-8 KJV).

Did you know that many of the greatest churches of the earth are churches that fast corporately? In my years of pastoral ministry, our greatest breakthroughs have come as we have fasted with our congregation.

BIBLE HEROES WHO FASTED

I have also noticed that many of the greatest Bible characters fasted. For instance, Ezra fasted before he made his journey back to Jerusalem. Feeling like it would be a lack of faith in God to ask the king for an armed escort, he said, "So we fasted, and God answered our prayer." I have chosen to follow this example on dozens of occasions to both my benefit and the benefit of the hundreds who have traveled with me throughout the earth.

Esther called for a three day fast before she approached the king concerning her antagonist, Haman. You see, Haman the hangman had devised a plan to eliminate the Jews, and Esther needed the favor of the king to make Haman's plan of no effect. The result of her awe-inspiring encounter: Haman was hanged on his own gallows. Oh, to live a life of fasting.

The three Hebrew boys in the Book of Daniel fasted, eating only pulse (dried peas and lentils) and water. They had refused to eat the king's food for ten days, and at the end of the ten days they looked fairer than all the rest of the captives. On a personal note, I have always fasted when traveling to foreign gospel-starved countries for ministry. I believe that the extraordinary results of that ministry time have been directly associated with prayer and fasting.

It is clear from The Lord's Prayer that we will need power to overcome the power of the enemy. This power comes as a direct result of our relationship with the Lord. He gives us authority in the earth as we submit to His authority. You know, I would hate to go to war with a squirrel gun. It is not wise to go through life ignorant of all Jesus has offered you in heavenly places. Consider the remarkable arsenal that is at your disposal in regards to spiritual warfare:

What then shall we say to these things? If God is for us, who is against us? (Rom. 8:31).

But in all these things we overwhelmingly conquer through Him who loved us (Rom. 8:37).

Put on the full armor of God, so that you will be able to stand firm against the schemes of the devil" (Eph. 6:11).

When He had disarmed the rulers and authorities, He made a public display of them, having triumphed over them through Him (Col. 2:15).

For the weapons of our warfare are not of the flesh, but divinely powerful for the destruction of fortresses (2 Cor. 10:4).

John, in his writing of 1 John 3:8b says, "The Son of God appeared for this purpose, to destroy the works of the devil." When you pray, you don't have to pray from a cast down position of weakness. But when you come boldly before the throne of grace, come from the position of one who has been seated in heavenly places with Christ Jesus!

I Am not Ashamed of a Gospel of Power

Throughout His ministry, Jesus continuously introduced his twelve disciples to the gospel that would be preached to the entire world for a witness of who He was. This gospel was accompanied with a power that would validate the message.

This gospel is a message about a King who lavishly gave us gifts so that we might overcome all the works of the enemy and be an extension of His mighty hand bringing glory to His name. Take care that you read this carefully: The world de-serves that we preach the gospel with power and demonstra-tion of the Spirit.

Don't rely solely on your clever ingenuity or religious rhetoric. Seek the things that are above. It is important to un-derstand that the message of the Kingdom must be accompa-nied the power of the Kingdom. Discover the power of His gifts of the Spirit—the gift of faith, the gift of the workings of miracles, and the gift of healings. These gifts of the Spirit can be released through prayer as well as all the other gifts of min-istration and ministry found in First Corinthians chapter 12. Again, we are admonished by the Lord to *earnestly* seek spiri-tual gifts. "Seek, and you shall find."

Jesus never intended that His model prayer become a magic prayer or a prayer of bondage. He desired that as we prayed this prayer *in faith*, looking to the Father, that the prayer would release the power they had by their relationship with Him. I firmly believe that when you pray this prayer, you are accessing the excess of what is available in God for your life today.

Jesus' message at His ascension into heaven was plain enough for His disciples to understand. They did not walk away from the place where the cloud took Him saying, "I won-der what He meant by that?" On the contrary, they went away expecting to receive power from on high, and they did just that. As one looks at the young church in the Book of Acts, he may be led to feel like this:

> Stirred because he is seeing Christianity, the real thing in action for the first time in human history. The new-born Church as vulnerable as any human child, having either money nor influence nor power in the ordinary sense, is setting forth joyfully and courageously to win the pagan world for God through Christ. The young

Church like all young creatures is appealing in its simplicity and single-heartedness. Here we are seeing the Church in its youth, valiant and unspoiled a body of ordinary men and women joined in an unconquerable fellowship never before seen in this earth.

But we cannot help feeling disturbed as well as moved, for this surely is the Church as it was intended to be. It is vigorous and flexible, for these are the days before it ever became fat and short of breath through prosperity, or muscle-bound by over-organization. These men did not make "acts of faith," they believed. They did not "say their prayers," they really prayed. They did not hold conferences in psychosomatic medicine, they simply healed the sick. But if they were uncomplicated and naïve by modern standards, we admit they were open to the God-ward side in a way that is almost unknown today.[3]

A dear friend of mine felt as though his ministry had dried up, and he simply could not figure out what was happening in his life. He had been used by God to start 157 Christian businessmen's chapters across the nation. He would make a cold call on a city and, when he left the city, there would be another chapter of men coming together to celebrate the love of Jesus. He was a man of deep insight into the things of God.

In 1961, he was in a hotel room in the South. He had prayed most of the day when, late into the night, the wall of the hotel room became a giant panoramic screen. Now, keep in mind this man had conducted evangelistic meetings where thousands had come and been saved, healed, and delivered. Still, he told me he was totally astonished at what was taking place right before his eyes. Looking at the wall, he suddenly saw an army that was fatigued and battle-weary. Their uniforms were torn and dirty, and the men themselves were in complete exhaustion. He said they were literally dragging their weapons of war.

Quick as a flash, the scene changed and he saw another army, polished and equipped. The second army came marching toward him on this giant screen. The army was resoundingly singing and marching in cadence. The bravery shown on their faces, and it was obviously a highly triumphant army. Before he had time to process all he had seen, an old rusty bolt appeared before him between the two armies. The man asked, "Lord, what is this?" The Lord then spoke to F. E. Ward and said, "The first army is those who have been fighting the battle up until now." "Lord," he asked, "what is this second army?" "The second army is what I am preparing to do in the earth." "Lord, what about the old rusty bolt?" The Lord spoke again, saying, "That is you, son. And, I want you to tie these two armies together."

F. E. Ward was a true father figure to hundreds of men and women of God. John Osteen and I conducted his funeral several years ago and, as we did, young and old men and women of God gathered to pay tribute to a man who had made his calling and election sure. It was this man who felt things were out of sorts. He called me and said, "Cleddie, something is not right. I seem to have lost the prophetic edge from my life." A few days later, he told me that he had found it. You see, he had let a minister's rejection get under his skin. It had been a man to whom he had been a great help, and the man has since gone on to have many fruitful years of ministry. However, F. E. was so sensitive that he went to this man and asked his forgiveness. The man was not even aware of the problem. But he, of course, asked for his friend's forgiveness and the power of God began to flow freely through his life as it had for many, many years.

God will not lead us into temptation, but we will find ourselves tested from time to time. In these times we must ask God to search our hearts. Then, we must make things right in Him. Be open to God. Be open to His Kingdom coming in your life. And remember, if we are to be used in releasing the captive, we must by necessity release others from any unforgiveness we may hold in our hearts. No pardon, no power.

> A major truth concerning temptation is that when temptation comes, it is already too late. The decision whether or not to yield to temptation has already been deeply influenced by prior decisions and by prior preparations for moral defense. Unless we arm ourselves in advance of the moral battle, we have very little chance when finally the actual test occurs. Professor John Baillie saw that watching and praying overlapped because, "prayer is the soul's vigil." Our best chance of escape from moral danger lies in the act of prayerful preparedness."[4]

CHAPTER TWELVE

Let the Praise of the Lord Be in My Mouth

For Thine is the kingdom, and the power, and the glory, for ever. Amen (Matt. 6:13b KJV).

Prayer is the passion for the secret places while worship is the passion for the high places. In the place of prayer man seeks that quiet place where he will be able to fervently speak to the Father in a way that His Son has taught men to pray. Jesus taught His friends that while they are praying, they end all prayers on a high note. From the secret place of unburdening their soul in prayer, they are now taught to rise on the wings of the Spirit and ascend into the high places of worship, praise, and adoration.

I will give thanks to the Lord according to His righteousness and will sing praise to the name of the Lord Most High (Ps. 7:17).

There is a river whose streams make glad the city of God, the holy dwelling places of the Most High (Ps. 46:4).

Who may ascend into the hill of the Lord? And who may stand in His holy place? (Ps. 24:3).

Joachim Jeremias says:

The doxology, "For thine is the kingdom and the power and the glory, for ever. Amen," is lacking completely in Luke, and in Matthew it is absent from the oldest manuscripts. We encounter it first in the Didache. But it would be a completely erroneous conclusion to suppose that The Lord's Prayer was ever prayed without some closing words of praise to God; in Palestinian practice it was completely unthinkable that a prayer would end with the word "temptation." Now, in Judaism prayers were often concluded with a "seal," a sentence of praise freely formulated by the man who was praying.

This was doubtless also what Jesus intended with The Lord's Prayer, and what the congregation did in the earliest period: conclude The Lord's Prayer with a "seal," i.e., a freely formulated doxology by the person praying. Afterwards, when The Lord's Prayer began to be used increasingly in the Service as a common prayer, it was felt necessary to establish a fixed formulation of the doxology.[1]

The Didache to which Jeremias is referring is an early, second-century, Christian composition. The "Teaching of the Twelve Apostles," as it is sometimes referred to, is a clear composite, consisting of a "Two Ways" section (chaps. 1-6), a liturgical manual (7-10), instructions on the reception of traveling prophets (11-15), and a brief apocalypse (16). Below is the portion of the Didache that quotes The Lord's Prayer as prayed in the second century. You will notice that the doxology is included.

> *8:5 Thy kingdom come;*
> *8:6 Thy will be done, as in heaven, so also on earth;*
> *8:7 give us this day our daily bread;*
> *8:8 and forgive us our debt, as we also forgive our debtors;*
> *8:9 and lead us not into temptation, but deliver us from the evil one;*
> *8:10 for Thine is the power and the glory for ever and ever.*
> *8:11 Three times in the day pray ye so.*

THE POWER OF PRAISE

There is nothing on the earth as powerful and inspiring as true, heartfelt praise. As worship rings out its melodious tunes down through the corridors of our heart, we immediately discover that we have been lifted up into those high places. When we fail to acknowledge the Lord in praise, we disregard how deserving He is of our utmost gratitude and appreciation. The goodness of the Lord is the foundation of all expressions of worship and praise. Those feelings of gratitude must be developed and expressed or our faith will waver and our prayers become shallow. Our Lord instructed those who were going to come into His presence with their prayers to begin and end all prayer with praise. Because of the power of praise, and since our heart is set on building our faith in regards to prayer, we should take into consideration what it means to praise the Lord. Listed below are the abbreviated definitions of seven different types of praise found in the Old Testament, taken from *How to Pray the Lord's Prayer.*

Each of these levels of praise show a different way in which to worship and glorify God. They include:

- *Todah*—which means "to extend hands in thanksgiving."

- *Yadah*—which means "to worship with extended hands/to throw out the hands enjoying God."
- *Hallal*—which means "to be vigorously excited; to laud, boast, rave, to celebrate."
- *Zamar*—which means "to pluck the strings of an instrument, to praise with song."
- *Barak*—which means "to bless; to declare God the origin of power for success, prosperity, and fertility; to be still."
- *Tehillah*—which means "singing in the spirit of singing hallals" (abandoned to one).
- *Shabach*—which means "to commend; to address in a loud tone; to shout."[2]

I HEAR A SOUND...

We are to enter into the gates of the great city of God with thanksgiving in our hearts, and as we arrive in those beautiful courts it is imperative to release the sounds of praise. For the past ten years, I have had the absolute delight of seeing a large part of the church experiencing a greater freedom and joy of expression when coming before God. I've found this liberty to be at a level I have only seen periodically in the past. I see the fire spreading. I feel the river rising. I hear the saints summoning, God's Kingdom to come!

Along with this revival of praise has come a new depth in intercession. Praise opens a man's heart to the purposes of God. In the atmosphere of worship, he forgets his desires as he is overwhelmed by the heart of God. The discord of selfish desire is replaced by heaven's rhythm, which is synchronized to the will of the Father. A worldwide emphasis on prayer has escalated throughout the Body of Christ because man's faith has been saturated by the "yes" and "amen" of the Holy Spirit.

I do not believe that you can separate the Siamese twins of praise and prayer. "Rejoice in the Lord, Oh you [uncompromisingly] righteous [you upright in right standing with God] for praise is becoming and appropriate for those who are upright in heart" (Ps. 33:1 AMP). The moment we begin to praise God we do what our adversary cannot do. Satan was once the chief musician in the heavenly courts, but he disqualified himself when he led a mutiny in heaven. Father has replaced him with the company of the saints. When we offer up sweet sounds of praise to our Father in heaven, we're doing the one thing hell cannot do—it cannot praise and worship God. Praise is *ours* to embrace. Prayers are *His* to answer in an exorbitant manner. *Through praise and prayer your insufficiency is swallowed up in His sufficiency.*

There are twelve different words for prayer in the Old Testament. In contrast to the Greek language, the Hebrew language is a picture language, and we will benefit tremendously by simply recognizing the diversity in the different words used to express what prayer can be. Prayer is like a diamond that has many facets, each blending together to complement the beauty of the piece. The diamond begins as a piece of coal, but the earth's pressure, over time, turns it into a very impregnable and valuable gem. This gem reflects light in greater dimensions than any other. Similarly, it may take four or five different words to define each word that is used for prayer.

PRAYER IS:

1. *Ana* and *Na*—These words together mean "a prayer of urgency." The Jews were offended by the transliteration of the word into *Hosanna,* which means, "Lord save us." Again, man's extremity is God's opportunity. I call it "prayer on the edge," such as Jacob holding on for dear life as he wrestled with the angel.

2. *Shaal*—This word usually means "to ask, to make enquiry or request." I have learned to be specific when I pray. We unwisely ask God for trivia when He invites us to ask for treasure. "Ask of Me, and I will surely give the nations as Your inheritance, and the very ends of the earth as Your possession" (Ps. 2:8).

3. *Chanan*—This means "the act of calling on another for assistance," and is often used in Psalms when God is called upon for aid. It is even used when God is said to make a person favorable or attractive in the eyes of another. This is the kind of prayer I have often prayed over the years.

4. *Athar* refers to prayers connected in part to burnt offerings. This prayer is typified as an aroma or fragrance. "May my prayer be counted as incense before You" (Ps. 141:2a).

One day, we walked into a department store with my son who was about three years old. We called him "Wild Kyle" during those years. Suddenly he was gone, which was par for the course. I could not see him, but I sure could smell him coming. In his excursion through the store, he had excitedly paused at the inviting fragrance counter. Faster than a pickpocket, he picked up a bottle and went to work. Dennis the Menace could have taken a lesson from him that day. In no time at all, the smell of fresh cut roses was all over him. A clerk with an unfriendly look on her face was in hot pursuit as he sought refuge with dear old Dad. You see, Kyle had taken a bottle of the latest fragrance and sprayed it all over himself and everyone else who came by. Needless to say, it was not difficult for me to find him for the rest of the day. He became like an identifiable aroma. Kyle became a good illustration of this prayer. It is perfumed prayer. As we pray in His name, all of heaven recognizes the fragrance of such an entreaty.

5. *Paga*— There is persistence in this word; it is a word of intervention. It is not the word used for those who dabble in prayer. Rather, it is a word for those who make faith contact God for the benefit of others. "But Ruth said, 'Do not *urge me* to leave you or turn back from following you; for where you go, I will go, and where you lodge, I will lodge. Your people shall be my people, and your God, my God' " (Ruth 1:16). *Paga* in this instance means, "press me not to leave you."

6. *Palal*—Found forty-eight times in the Old Testament, it is a word thought to come from the Aramaic, which meant "to notch the edge of a sword." When it is used in Scripture it means" to assess, to estimate, to break one's self, to abhor one's self, to confess, or actually be in self-judgment." It is the kind of prayer used in the act of personal repentance on Daniel's part when he identifies with the need of Israel in Babylonian captivity.

7. *Tsela*—Daniel was a man of prayer. "He kneeled upon his knees three times a day and prayed [*tsela*], as was his custom" (see Dan. 6:10). He lowered himself before the Lord. And, when we humble ourselves under the mighty hand of God, He will lift us up. You see, Daniel had been forbidden not to pray to anyone other than King Darius for thirty days at the threat of being thrown into a lion's den. The trap was set, because those who had devised this plan knew Daniel had a consistent prayer life. The

difference was, Daniel could pray prayers that shut lion's mouths and they could not.

8. *Tephillah*—This is the prayer of the individual. What you and I want most to hear after we pray is that God has heard our prayer. This prayer refers to making supplication like Job did when he prayed, "pity me, pity me." This prayer is used over thirty times in the Book of Psalms and seventy-one times in the Old Testament over all. "I have heard your prayer and have chosen this place for Myself as a house of sacrifice. If I shut up the heavens...and My people who are called by My name humble themselves and pray and [seek, crave, and require of necessity] My face and turn from their wicked ways, then I will hear from heaven" (2 Chron. 7:12b-14a).

9. *Chalah* means "to smooth or make sweet the face of someone." *Strong's Enhanced Hebrew Dictionary* defines it as "an humble request with no commanding or demanding." Considering that Christ's countenance was prophesied to be marred—and was marred—more than any other man's in all of history, you want to stroke His face in prayer. Lavish your love upon Him. We should keep this in mind.

10. *Lachash*—Some translators call this a secret prayer or sigh. It is a prayer offered up that is only a whisper. It is found in this verse, "They poured out a prayer when...chastening was upon them"(Isa. 26:166 KJV) I recommend you not live without one of these prayers.

11. *Siach*—This word means "to meditate, complain, commune, or to muse." I have to be honest here; I have done quite a bit of each of these over the years.

Ward Chandler once told me, "I have cried enough tears in unbelief to float a battleship."

George Mueller, the great man of prayer, confessed there was a time when he would pray and then read the Word of God; but in later days he would read the Word of God and then pray that word into his heart.[3]

12. *Baah* is a word that means "to cause to swell, or boil up." Have you ever had a prayer boil up inside you? I have seen both churches and believers bulging with prayer. The prophet Isaiah uses this word when he prays, "Oh, that You would rend the heavens and come down...You did awesome things which we did not expect" (Isa. 64:1-3a). This kind of praying is igniting prayer, prayer that will heat up to 212 degrees Fahrenheit. You can take the temperature of a prayer meeting just like you can an individual. This kind of prayer will cause you to expect the unexpected, not just *expect the inspected.*

No wonder the disciples asked that the Lord would teach them to pray! How much have we missed by not understanding the different ways we can approach God's throne in the posture of prayer? We are not to remain dormant. Rather, we are to grow from glory to glory, embracing wisdom and praising His name forever!

"For *Thine* is the *kingdom* and the *power* and the *glory forever.*" The Lord encourages us to begin and end with praise as we pray like He prayed. We are to follow His example in all things. Paul admonished the church at Thessalonica to give thanks in everything.

FROM PRISON TO PRAISE

I remember a television interview I did with Merlin Carrothers, the author of the best selling book *Prison to Praise*. At the time of the interview, Merlin had just received a letter from a man who had read his book. The man was incarcerated for a horrible crime, and he, in his own testimony, told how he was at one point so violent and uncontrollable that he had been placed in solitary confinement. While in that despicable place, one of the guards gave him Merlin's book, *Prison to Praise*. The man had nothing else to do with his dreadful time, so he read it. And, as he read the book, he did not believe a word he read.

Then his heart changed. He began to praise God for the prison, the warden, the cockroaches, and the guards whom he hated and who hated him. When his days in solitary confinement were finally over, these guards came to release him. However, when they opened the solid cell door, he was so changed they did not believe he was the same man.

> For the beauty of nature, the fellowship of the good, the tender love of home; for safe conduct in temptation, strength to overcome, deliverance from evil; for the generousness, the patience, the sympathy of God; and for ten thousand-thousand unobserved or unremembered mercies, let us unweariedly bless His Holy Name. 'Oh, Give thanks to the Lord for He is good; for his mercies endure forever (Psalms 136:1).'[4]

This is how I pray the Lord's model prayer:

- **I make a declaration that I am God's child and He is my Heavenly Father, knowing that He will not turn His child away.**
- **I declare that His name is holy, and I then exalt the seven Old Testament names of God over every area**

164

of my life and over the needs of my family and friends.

- **I pray for my life priorities to be aligned with His will for my life in my home and church.**
- **I pray for the replenishing and the provision of daily bread, for seed to the sower and bread to the eater.**
- **I pray for pardon and the power to forgive, and for the power of forgiveness to be in the hearts of fellow believers.**
- **I pray for power in my life to overcome temptation, and I pray that those I serve and love will do the same.**
- **I praise Him for His coming Kingdom, power and glory forever! (This is a prayer of proclamation.)**

In closing, you must never forget that this book was never meant to be a "how-to" book. It is simply an "add-to" book, meaning that my faith is adding to your life in regards to the limitless possibilities in praying His prayer. Throughout the years, this prayer model has invariably kept me on track and always ready for the unexpected. We have prayed up buildings, churches, Christian businesses, and finances for workers' houses and land. We have prayed out harvesters and workers into the vast field of the world. And, we have prayed in co-workers and laborers into the vineyard.

This is the autobiography of a prayer life, and it all began when I prayed with my senior pastor that memorable week in the winter of 1972. As a result, my life has never been the same. Pray "Thy kingdom come!" And when it comes, you will find yourself side by side with thousands of men and women who have discovered the power in this effectual prayer. Be a doer of the Word, and you will find yourself praying the Lord's model prayer just as we have. "Let the high praises of God be in their mouth, and a two-edged sword in their hand" (Ps. 149:6).

If one ventures to summarize in one phrase the inexhaustible mystery of the few sentences in The Lord's Prayer, there is an expression pre-eminently suitable, which New Testament research has especially busied itself with in recent decades.

> That phrase is "eschatology becoming actualized." This expression denotes the age of salvation now being realized, the consummation bestowed **in advance, the "in-breaking" of God's presence into our lives.** Where men dare to pray in the name of Jesus to their heavenly Father with childlike trust, that he might reveal his glory and that he might grant to them, already today and in this place the bread of life and the blotting out of sins, there in the midst of the constant threat of failure and apostasy is realized, already now, the kingly rule of God over the life of his children.[5]

Your prayers, as have mine, may range from desperation to a whisper, but the prayer is there nonetheless, ascending from our lips to the throne room of the Father. God has given us a standing invitation to come boldly to His throne of grace. I daily take Him up on His offer, and I pray that you will also join me in this prayer:

> *Our Father which art in heaven, Hallowed be Thy name.*
> *Thy kingdom come. Thy will be done in earth, as it is in heaven.*
> *Give us this day our daily bread. And forgive us our debts, as we forgive our debtors.*
> *And lead us not into temptation, but deliver us from evil:*
> *For Thine is the kingdom, and the power, and the glory, for ever. Amen* (Matt. 6:9-13 KJV).

Endnotes

Introduction

1. Frank C. Laubach, *Prayer: the Mightiest Force in the World* (Old Tappan, NJ: Spirit Books, ©1959).

2. Joachim Jeremias, *The Lord's Prayer* (Philadelphia, PA: Fortress Press, ©1964).

3. http://www.ccel.org/w/watson/prayer/prayer.txt

4. http://www.cwo.com/~pentrack/catholic/francis1.html

Chapter 1

1. E.M. Bounds, *The Necessity of Prayer* (Grand Rapids, MI: Baker Books, ©1976), 37.

2. S.D. Gordon, *Quiet Talks on Prayer* (Shippensburg, PA: MercyPlace, a division of Destiny Image Publishers, ©2003),153.

Chapter 2

1. S.D. Gordon, *Quiet Talks on Prayer* (Shippensburg, PA: MercyPlace, a division of Destiny Image Publishers, ©2003), 10–11.

2. E.M. Bounds, *The Possibilities of Prayer* (Grand Rapids, MI: Baker Books, ©1979), 34.

3. Ibid. 43.

CHAPTER 3

1. J. Sidlow Baxter, *Majesty* (San Bernadino, CA: Here's Life Publishers, ©1984), 169.

2. Clarence E. Macartney, D.D., *The Lord's Prayer* (New York, NY: Fleming H. Revell Company, © 1952), 158.

3. International Bible Translators, Inc., *The Great Book: The Plain English Bible* (Shippensburg, PA: Destiny Image Publishers, 2003.

4. Joaquim Jeremias, *The Lord's Prayer* (Philadelphia, PA: Fortress Press, ©1964), 19.

5. Hallesby, *Prayer* (Minneapolis, MN: Augsburg Publishing House, ©1931).

6. John Allan Lavender, *Why Prayers are Unanswered* (Valley Forge, PA: Judson Press, ©1967).

7. Don Milam, *Lost Passions of Jesus* (Shippensburg, PA: Mercy Place a division of Destiny Image Publishers, ©1999), 99.

CHAPTER 4

1. T. Austin-Sparks, *Pioneers of the Heavenly Way* (Gaithersburg, MD: Testimony Book Ministry n.d.), 9.

2 IBID.

3. Rosalind Rinker, *PRAYER: Conversing With God* (Grand Rapids, MI: Zondervan Publishing House, © 1959).

4. http://skyways.lib.ks.us/poetry/fetzer/ofather.html

CHAPTER 5

1. Don Milam, *Lost Passions of Jesus* (Shippensburg, PA: MercyPlace, a division of Destiny Image Publishers, ©1998),16-17.

2. Bill Johnson, *When Heaven Invades Earth* (Shippensburg, PA: Destiny Image Publishers, ©2003),41.

3. Reginald E.O. White, *Prayer Is the Secret* (Harper Brothers, © 1958).

CHAPTER 6

1. Living Classics author John Bunyan, edited by Louis Gifford Parkhurst, Jr., *PILGRIMS PRAYER BOOK* (Wheaton, IL: Tyndale House Publishers, compiled from original works written in 1662, published in 1986).

2. S. D. Gordon, *Quiet Talks on Prayer* (Shippensburg, PA: MercyPlace, a division of Destiny Image Publishers,©2003), 14, 5.

3. Matthew 7:21.

4. International Bible Translators, Inc., *The Great Book: The Plain English Bible* (Shippensburg, PA: Destiny Image Publishers, ©2003).

5. Andrew Murray, *With Christ in the School of Prayer* (Old Tappan, NJ: Print Basis Fleming H. Revell, ©1953), 30.

6. http://www.quotedb.com/quotes/594

CHAPTER 7

1. http://www.digiserve.com/mystic/Christian/resources/prayer/Lords_prayer/Chrysostom/

CHAPTER 8

1. Andrew Murray, *With Christ in the School of Prayer*, Old Tappan, NJ: Print Basis Flemin H. Revell, © 1953).

2. Joachim Jeremias, *The Lord's Prayer*, (Philadelphia, PA: Fortress Press, ©1964), 22.

3. International Bible Translators, Inc., *The Great Book: The Plain English Bible* (Shippensburg, PA: Destiny Image Publishers, ©2003).

4. Ibid.

5. Alan Redpath, *Victorious Praying* (3 Beggarwood Lane, Basingstoke, Hants, United Kingdom: Pickering & Inglis n.d.), 13.

CHAPTER 9

1. International Bible Translators, Inc., *The Great Book: The Plain English Bible* (Shippensburg, PA: Destiny Image Publishers, ©2003).

2. Ibid.

3. R. Arthur Matthew, *Born for Battle* (Littleton, CO: OMF Books n.d.).

4. J. Oswald Sanders, *Prayer Power Unlimited* (Minneapolis, MN: Billy Graham Evangelistic Association n.d.), 98.

5. Joachim Jeremias, *The Lord's Prayer* Philadelphia, PA: Fortress Press, ©1964), 23-24.

CHAPTER 10

1. Joachim Jeremias, *The Lord's Prayer* (Philadelphia, PA: Fortress Press, ©1964), 28.

2. Praying the Lord's Prayer, Bible Prayer Card. Used by permission of Pastor Bob Rodgers. Evangel World Prayer Center, Louisville, Kentucky.

CHAPTER 11

1. http://www.studylight.org/com/bnn/view.cgi?book= mt&chapter=006

2. Joachim Jeremias, *The Lord's Prayer* (Philadelphia, PA: Fortress Press, ©1964), 29.

3. J. B. Phillips, *The Young Church in Action* (Great Britain: Fontana Books, 1953), 11.

4. Elton Trueblood, *The Lord's Prayer* (New York, NY: Harper and Row, ©1965), 60.

CHAPTER 12

1. Joachim Jeremias, *The Lord's Prayer* (Philadelphia, PA: Fortress Press,©1964), 28.

2. *How to Pray The Lord's Prayer* (Louisville, KY: Bob Rodgers Ministries, ©2000).

3. F. E. Marsh, *Major Bible Truths: Structural Principles of the Bible* (Glasgow, Scotland: Pickering & Inglis n.d.).

4. David M. MacIntryre, *The Hidden Life of Prayer* (Houston, TX: Christian Focus Publications, ©1989), 53.

5. Joachim Jeremias, *The Lord's Prayer* (Philadelphia, PA: Fortress Press, ©1964), 32-33.

CONTACT INFORMATION

To contact the author you may write or call him at:

CLEDDIE KEITH

HERITAGE FELLOWSHIP

7216 Highway 42

Florence, KY 41042

PH: 859-525-1124

E-mail: CLEDDIE@aol.com

ALSO BY CLEDDIE KEITH

PRAYING THE TEN COMMANDMENTS

Have you ever thought why we should celebrate the Ten Commandments? What does the Ten Commandments and prayer have in common?

Cleddie Keith lifts the Ten Commandments out of their natural habitat as a legal document and presents them as powerful truths that will motivate the believer towards prayer. Keith creatively shifts the focus from 'keeping' the Ten Commandments to 'praying' the Ten Commandments. Looking at each commandment the author supplies fuel to motivate the reader in his life of prayer. This is not a textbook...it is a prayer book and the Ten Commandments will never be the same again.

ISBN 0-7684-3016-X

Additional copies of this book and other
book titles from DESTINY IMAGE are
available at your local bookstore.

For a complete list of our titles,
visit us at www.destinyimage.com
Send a request for a catalog to:

Destiny Image® Publishers, Inc.
P.O. Box 310
Shippensburg, PA 17257-0310

*"Speaking to the Purposes of God for This
Generation and for the Generations to Come"*